Learning Packages in American Education

Learning Packages in American Education

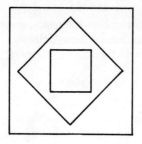

Philip G. Kapfer
and
Miriam B. Kapfer
Editors

Educational Technology Publications
Englewood Cliffs, New Jersey 07632

Library of Congress Cataloging in Publication Data

Kapfer, Miriam B
    Learning packages in American education.

    1. Individualized instruction—Addresses, essays,
lectures. 2. Educational innovations—United
States—Addresses, essays, lectures. I. Kapfer,
Philip G., joint author. II. Title.
LB1031.K35   371.39'4   72-11507
ISBN 0-87778-047-1

The contents of this book were printed originally in the September, 1972 issue of *Educational
Technology* Magazine.

Copyright © 1972 Educational Technology
Publications, Englewood Cliffs, New Jersey
07632.

Printed in the United States of America.

Library of Congress Catalog Card Number:
72-11507

International   Standard   Book   Number:
0-87778-047-1

First Printing: January, 1973.

Table of Contents

Learning Packages in American Education

Introduction to Learning Packages

Philip G. Kapfer and Miriam B. Kapfer

A confusing array of alternative approaches to packaged learning exists on the educational scene. Many claim to be effective means for individualizing instruction for students. Others do not mention individualization, but in fact are individualized. And still other packages are specifically designed for teacher-conducted group instruction and yet contain some elements similar to those included in packages designed for individualization. Viewed in perhaps the simplest way, individualized instruction and/or learning packages are systematized ways of delivering content and process to learners.

Rationale for the Book

In preparing this book, each contributor was asked to consider, if possible, the following two questions in his chapter:

(1) How do you resolve the standard problems and issues in curriculum development, such as the following:
  (a) What should be the goals of the school?
  (b) What educational experiences are most likely to promote attainment of these goals?
  (c) How can such educational experiences be organized most effectively?
  (d) How can the attainment of these goals be measured?
(2) How do you materialize the curriculum?
  (a) What format(s) do you use for your materials?
  (b) What curricular components are included in your

3

packages for the student? For the teacher?

(c)   Who develops the materials?

(d)   How are the curriculum developers trained?

(e)   How are teachers and students trained to use your packages?

(f)   What kinds of support services (e.g., library, community, administrative, etc.) are needed to properly implement the use of your packages by students?

Of course, these are only a few of the topics to which contributors addressed themselves. Some covered more of these than others, and some felt that many of these questions did not apply to their particular curricular activity or kind of package. In any case, the authors were asked to give enough information about their particular learning packages so that readers could make intelligent choices from among the alternatives.

Individualized Instruction and Learning Packages

Definitions of individualized instruction and of learning packages abound, and differ considerably from one person to the next. We will leave to each author in this book his own definitions, but wish to provide the reader with at least a partial means of sorting out the definitions and the examples.

Individualized instruction commonly includes one or more of the following elements:

(1)   Provision for variability among students in the *rate* at which they are able to achieve a desired degree of mastery of a given behavior.

(2)   Provision for variability among students in the *"skills"* (e.g., reading, writing, using audio-visual equipment, etc.) that they possess at a given point in time and, therefore, their *readiness* for employing these skills as tools for using various learning materials and activities.

(3)   Provision for variability among students in their *knowledge, understanding* and *attitude development* along a continuum ranging from simple perception to the

highest levels of understanding and value development (choice of action).

(4) Provision for variability among students in their *verbal development* (e.g., ranging from "show and tell" to understandably communicating complex ideas).

(5) Provision for variability among students in their *motor skill development* (e.g., ranging from random movement to using precision, control, grace or speed of movement).

(6) Provision for variability among students in *responsibility development* (e.g., self-direction, self-initiative, self-discipline, willingness to put forth effort, or willingness to follow oral or written instructions and standard operating procedures) along a continuum from external (teacher) shaping of these behaviors to conscious (student) valuing and choosing these behaviors.

(7) Provision for variability among students in readiness for *self-motivated learning* (e.g., based on immediate academic, in-life or career goals that each student wants).

At the same time, in packaged (or unpackaged) instructional materials and activities, concern is commonly demonstrated for one or more of the following elements:

(1) Provision for variability in societal, parental and student *expectations* concerning the subject matter and behaviors to be learned.

(2) Provision for variability in *interactions* among students, between students and teachers and between students and materials.

(3) Provision for variability of *subject matter* in forms (from concrete to abstract) and in formats (books, films, objects, discussions, etc.) that most efficiently and effectively support the behaviors being sought.

(4) Provision for variability in *instructional settings* (whether for individual students or for groups of students) in which interactions can take place, subject matter can be learned and behaviors can be practiced.

(5) Provision for the *motivational appeal* of the interactions, materials and settings.

There are obviously degrees to which instructional materials and activities can be individualized and/or packaged. For example, if a group of students and teachers are engaged in setting up simulated political conventions for the purpose of nominating presidential candidates from each political party, time constraints common to all of the students will have to be placed on the learning packages that contain the subject matter to be learned while planning the simulation. Such constraints are necessary in order for the students to practice the desired behaviors during the scheduled conventions. However, variability among students in learning skills, conceptual-affective development, verbal development, motor skill development and level of responsibility can be taken into account in the learning packages that are provided, as well as in the tasks for which each student is responsible, both before and during the simulated conventions. The learning package approaches represented in this book necessarily reflect considerations such as these.

Contents of the Book

Several authors describe learning packages that are related to the type of "Individualized Learning Packages" (ILPs) for which Philip G. Kapfer and Glen F. Ovard give detailed information and construction procedures in their book titled *Preparing and Using Individualized Learning Packages for Ungraded, Continuous Progress Education* (Educational Technology Publications, 1971). Kapfer and Ovard, and (represented in this book) Swenson, Dalton and J. Smith were involved in the early development and dissemination of what became known as the I/D/E/A (Kettering Foundation) UNIPAC. Interesting variations can be seen, of course, in the development procedures, implementation suggestions, and other points of emphasis included by these contributors. Feild and Swenson, for example, sketch the current UNIPAC format and discuss the effectiveness of UNIPAC workshops in promoting in teachers the attitudes and skills conducive to individualization. Dalton describes a simplified, one-page individualized learning package developed for the Alhambra (California)

Schools called the "Learning Model." The "Learning Activity Package" (LAP) is defined as to purpose and content by Smith. Unlike many of the other authors represented in this book, however, Smith does not look upon the LAP as "exportable" from one school district to another, but rather suggests that each district must write all of its own LAPs.

The learning packages described by Flanagan, Esbensen, Bolvin and Burns, although developed independently of the UNIPAC, are similar to it in certain component elements and uses. Flanagan provides a longitudinal look at the rationale for and contents of the Teaching-Learning Units (TLUs) contained in the PLAN system for individualization developed by the American Institutes for Research. Also described are the PLAN curricular support systems, including student guidance, teacher training, and computer functions. A complete example of a Duluth "Student Learning Contract" is provided by Esbensen. Following a discussion of Contract components, he suggests several applications of the Contract system, including the "family decision-making" approach. Bolvin discusses the work of the Learning Research and Development Center at the University of Pittsburgh within the context of current widespread efforts toward educational goal setting. Specifically reported are the development procedures and components of packages in the Individually Prescribed Instruction program (IPI). Burns titles the learning packages developed for use at the University of Texas (El Paso) as "Instructional Modules." He details the essential components of IMs and suggests possible methods for using them.

The Born-Zlutnick and Postlethwait-Hurst chapters represent attempts to individualize instruction at the university level through semi-programmed course materials. Born and Zlutnick describe in operational terms an instructional delivery model based on Keller's "Personalized System of Instruction." In PSI, the curricular content is made available to the student in written form. Individualized as to rate, PSI is designed to guarantee content mastery for the student who possesses enough self-discipline to stick to his studies. The Audio-Tutorial packages and system originally developed for botany courses at Purdue University are presented by Postlethwait and Hurst. In the AT approach, emphasis is placed on providing a range of types of learning materials including tapes, slides and pertinent realia. Of special interest is the authors' description of two recent additions to the AT system—the concepts of minicourses and mastery learning.

Competency-based teacher education is an umbrella-like term currently at the forefront of educational interest. In general, such programs are individualized, field centered, and based on specific performance criteria. Bechtol outlines the competency-based program at Southwest Minnesota State College as well as the "ComPacs" that have been developed to implement the program. In the Burke chapter, the Weber Individualized Learning Kits (WILKITs) that comprise the competency-based teacher education program at Weber State College are described.

Also in the teacher education field, but primarily at the in-service level, are packaged materials described by a number of other authors. Packages for the in-service development of special education teachers are the focus of the Baum-Chastain chapter. Howell reports on the TULSAPAC, a package design that was used initially for the in-service education of administrators and teachers in Tulsa, Oklahoma. He also describes the type of in-service activities that show promise for bringing the TULSAPAC into general use with children in Tulsa classrooms.

Program 100, under development by the Northwest Regional Educational Laboratory, is focused on the improvement of selected teacher competencies. Of central concern to Program 100 developers has been the dynamic nature of today's world and, consequently, the type of educational reformation required by ever-present change. Jung provides an account of the typical content of the packaged Program 100 instructional systems. Borg details the development process, format and content of "Mini-courses," individualized multimedia learning packages for teacher education developed by the Far West Laboratory for Educational Research and Development.

Kapfer and Woodruff present a comprehensive "Life-Involvement Model" (LIM) of curriculum and instruction that is applicable at all educational levels. Descriptions are included of the psychological basis for the model, as well as of the three types of learning packages through which the model is applied—"Carrier Projects," "Units" and "Ventures." Inherent in the LIM approach is a rigorous and well-developed curricular structure that results in serious-minded but functional learning. At a time when at least one branch of educational thinkers is calling for the total elimination from society of schools as we know them, Kapfer and Woodruff propose equally strong medicine for the ills of education, but without the result of killing the patient.

The chapters by Corwin and Madeja present attempts to package materials for learning, but *not* to "build curricula." The "Discovery Boxes" described by Corwin are developed for loan by the staff of the Children's Museum in Boston. Focused on real-life phenomena, they represent a step away from teacher-dominated learning and a step toward productive, small-group exploration by learners. Corwin points out that such kits are designed to accommodate at least two different learning styles—the "linear learner" and the "messer-about." Corwin states that Discovery Boxes are not intended "for specific teaching of curriculum content," but rather for extending learning experiences in diverse ways. Madeja describes four categories of primary level packages being developed by the Aesthetic Education Program of the Central Midwestern Regional Educational Laboratory (CEMREL). The packages are designed to transcend the individual arts by focusing on universal aesthetic phenomena, such as "organizing art elements" and "transforming art elements into end products that communicate." Madeja states that the CEMREL packages are "not conceived of as *a* curriculum, but as a resource for the development of curricula."

Reserved for the final positions in this book are two chapters that are not about packages *per se* at all. These chapters, by Tosti and Harmon and by Smith and Kapfer, provide context for many of the package systems described by other authors in this book. Tosti and Harmon discuss techniques of individualizing instruction in terms of a taxonomy of instructional management. They define individualized instruction as a function of the frequency of the decision to change instructional presentations as a result of assessing student behavior.

Examining instructional management from a different direction, Smith and Kapfer present student management techniques for "living with" packages and individualized instruction in the classroom. Too frequently, teachers who make the shift from traditional instructional materials and group-paced approaches to learning packages and individualized approaches experience difficult and unnecessary behavior problems on the part of students. Reinforcement techniques, appropriately applied, are critical for establishing an effective learning climate and a new set of standard operating procedures. Thus, the Smith-Kapfer chapter is designed to help the classroom teacher shape the self-directing behaviors in students that are required by many of the packaged materials and approaches contained in this book.

Philip G. Kapfer and **Miriam B. Kapfer** are at the University of Utah, Salt Lake City, in the Bureau of Educational Research and The Center to Improve Learning and Instruction, respectively. Philip Kapfer is a Contributing Editor.

The UNIPAC: A Form and Process for Individualizing

William B. Feild and Gardner Swenson

Beyond the basic skills, the three Rs, there is little consensus among educators as to what should constitute the curriculum in the schools. If there ever was consensus, it is doubtful that there ever will be again. Knowledge simply does not come across the horizon anymore in convenient, priority-laden doses, but rather comes in great masses of continuous, undifferentiated input which, as Whitehead said, keeps about as well as fresh fish.

There is more agreement as to what the student should *be able to do* than as to what he should know. Authorities and lay persons alike are coming to believe that beyond the student's possession of a number of eclectic facts and basic processes commensurate with those of the average student around him, the student must now possess certain skills and characteristics which are more important to him than "knowledge" as traditionally defined. These skills and characteristics are as follows:

1. The student must possess the skills to do significant and accelerated research.
2. The student must know how (and be able) to manipulate the learning environment.
3. The student must be able to "re-specialize" in alien fields on short notice and without anxiety or insecurity.

The control of students by teachers and by the system changes in an individualized program. The student's role becomes harder, more responsible, less dependent; the teacher's role becomes softer, more objective, more professional (diagnostic-prescriptive); the system's role becomes service oriented rather

11

than authoritarian, so that the barriers of department, time, space, process and material give way to teacher-student planned subsystems to support learning.

Any organization which will effectively support this kind of educational experience must first establish beyond doubt that the individual student is a known entity, that his goals are relevant, and that he knows and understands what his goals are. Secondly, the organization must provide the student with meaningful choices, and must guarantee access to these goals through the student's own efforts. Thirdly, the organization must provide the student with a legitimate means of exercising these choices and of knowing when he has reached his objectives. Finally, the organization must allow him to move at his own speed. Consistent with these assumptions (and indeed inherent in them!) are the legal responsibilities of teachers, the acquisition of self-knowledge by the student, and Bloom's assumption that 90 percent of the students in this country could make "A" in any subject, regardless of the criteria for "A," if they were given *time,* the *proper process,* and the predisposition toward individualized instruction.

In the past we have evaluated school programs by matching the achievement scores of students against the hundreds of thousands of scores through which such tests are standardized. It would be far more significant, however, if we could evaluate success by measuring the number of objectives achieved, by the holding power of the school, by the degree to which the school changed in all its aspects, by the satisfaction of the incumbents, by some measure of decreased neurotic adults, decreased crime, fewer broken families, or fewer welfare recipients, or by the increased joy of life held by the next generation.

UNIPAC Format

The UNIPAC was designed to satisfy the goals and conditions outlined above. As a package, a lesson plan, a systems approach, or the material for individualizing instruction, the UNIPAC is not readily distinguished by its format from other packages. It contains the classic package elements and its power lies in its utilization. The package format is as follows:

1. *Pre-test*—designed to determine readiness, prerequisites, and student need for the lesson.
2. *Main concept*—stated in a declarative sentence and related to a time element to be discussed later.
3. *Component Parts* (parts to be learned)—stated in words or phrases to limit the otherwise limitless scope of any declarative sentence.
4. *The behavioral objectives*—written behaviorally with major emphasis on performance and conditions of performance and minor emphasis on level of proficiency. Related directly to terminal performance desired regarding each component.
5. *Instructions for selection of activities*—the first element of a recycling device to be discussed later.
6. *The diversified activities*—three or more per objective, diversified for entry and access rather than for reinforcement (may reinforce, however).
7. *The self-test*—a decision point for the student and a protection against public failure.
8. *Post-test*—identical to the objectives, the teacher's portion of the mutual contract.
9. *Quest*—the opportunity to go beyond the objectives learned, under any condition which will be profitable to the student.
10. *The field test*—an application of the package to determine its success and usefulness.

Several key features may be observed here which distinguish the UNIPAC from other learning packages:

(1) The main idea is a single concept, a manageable idea extracted from the unit, and the component parts are selected from among *all possible* component parts. The selection is a teacher-choice and tends to limit the expected time required to complete the package to ten days for senior high and three days for elementary. Although times will vary, of course, these limits represent the points at which anxiety and need for closure result in a sudden drop in student performance and an increase in boredom reactions. It is a clue for teacher intervention to check

again for lacking prerequisites, or for package weaknesses. The main idea, components and objectives are non-instructional; that is, they are stated in basic terms in order to help the student focus on and organize the task before him. If the components are divergent or the objectives numerous, the package is divided into several lessons, each with a self-test to help achieve closure.

(2) The recycling device is brought into play with the instructions for the *selection* of learning activities. The teacher has controlled the process and the goals to this point and is now turning responsibility over to the student, who may choose from among the activities only those he needs to pass the self-test. The activity choices are diversified rather than simply multiplied. This is done so that, regardless of the student's liabilities or learning specialties, he is likely to be able to reach the objectives with *minimum* teacher intervention. This diversification varies the form of presentation or involvement (and thus the learning mode) so that the same material may be presented in a number of ways. Reinforcement patterns may also evolve. The student makes choices based on his best or most enjoyable way of learning. He ceases making choices and performing activities when he has reached his objective (which he knows from the self-test data). If he fails the self-test, he has new activities from which to choose. This choice not only allows him to accept and exercise responsibility, but also helps him learn what his best way of learning is, an invaluable personal possession. In other types of packages, in which he is given no choice, his failure at the self-test level merely requires him to repeat the same activities from which he has not learned before!

(3) The quest element allows the student latitude to establish his own goals, to exhibit his research skills, and to demonstrate his ability to control his own time. This allows the instructor to capitalize on the student's already positive motivation.

UNIPAC Workshops

Teachers are trained to develop UNIPACs in workshops which are individualized, product oriented, and which use the UNIPAC format and philosophy in teaching teachers how to make

UNIPACs. The UNIPAC responds to the local curriculum. Packages are made using the concepts of the locally used scope and sequence. At the point where all concepts are packaged, the program becomes continuous progress. Succeeding packages developed between and among these laterally organized concepts give a vertical character which responds totally to individual differences. Until a number of packages are available to the teacher, he simply begins with one dependable student, continues to teach the others as he has, and expands the program to them slowly as he develops it. Any learning activity, book, kit, medium, machine or process available to the school becomes a legitimate activity choice in the package.

All of the more than 5,000 UNIPACs in the national UNIPAC bank were prepared by teachers for particular students who are identified by characteristics which were important to each teacher. Each package contains the student section, teacher section, and field test results. These 5,000 UNIPACs are available at cost in paper form or in microfiche to participating teachers.

Summary

The form and elements of the UNIPAC lead to performance, and the application of the UNIPAC process leads to individualization. This process ultimately requires a "conspiracy" with scheduling, administration, space, organization, etc., in order to reach its full effectiveness, but even alone the UNIPAC fosters an irresistable tendency toward quality in education.

William B. Feild is President, W.B. Feild and Associates, Kendall, Florida. **Gardner Swenson** is Director, Teachers' UNIPAC Exchange, Salt Lake City, Utah.

The Single-Page Learning Model

Leonard F. Dalton

The Learning Model adopted in Alhambra, California, is the result of eight years of research and development by former Kettering I/D/E/A consultants who worked with teachers throughout the world to produce a variety of independent, personalized curriculum products of a performance design. The individualized learning package developed for the Alhambra schools is a simplified one-page Learning Model that contains all of the components, but not the bulk, of the original learning package design. Formerly, the time needed for a teacher to prepare one of the first-generation learning packages was equivalent to that required by a typical three-credit-hour graduate course. Using the new model, the teacher can produce 30 packages in the same amount of time.

The Learning Model can best be defined as a simplified communication device that allows individual teacher and student diagnosis and prescription. If one follows this model, course challenges and partial credit contracts at the secondary level become truly meaningful. Learning strategies, such as large group lectures, small discussion groups and independent study, take on a new image, because they can now be scheduled as needed, rather than as dictated by a confining master schedule.

Components of the Learning Model

The SUBJECT is the first item in the Learning Model. Information in this category is used as a means of classification. In addition to the subject classification, it is wise to develop an internal school code for concept sequence identification (as shown

16

Subject:

Concept:

Purpose:

Objectives:

Pretest: If you think you can do the above objectives, obtain a pretest from
   your teacher. The following activities are suggested to you as ways to
   achieve the objectives:
Learning Activities: (May be selected by you or assigned by your teachers.)

Posttest: After completing the learning activities, ask your teacher for the
   posttest.
Quest Suggestions: Since you passed the pretest, you need not do the learning
   activities. You may wish to go on to the next learning package or study
   an activity of your own choosing such as:

Figure 1

Learning Model

in the sample Learning Model in Figure 1).

The CONCEPT or idea to be learned is in reality the title of the Learning Model. It should contain little or no factual data. Although a complete positive statement is preferable, it may also be written in an open-ended or question form if the author prefers.

The PURPOSE or rationale is the *why* of the Model. If teachers are not experienced at writing such statements, it can be a difficult task. Many segments of curriculum have been eliminated due to teachers' experiencing difficulty in writing rationale statements for them. Teachers who would avow that the entire educational structure of a school would fall if certain segments of their course were deleted have been known to eliminate volun- tarily many of these same segments when they were asked to write a rationale for why that part of the curriculum should be learned.

The OBJECTIVES are the observable performance that is expected of the pupil as evidence that a given concept has been learned. Experience has demonstrated that it is wise to write such statements *to* the student, i.e., in the second person. This procedure is recommended for all grade levels, even for the nonreader, for the simple reason that any teacher aide will now possess a built-in script to use directly with the student or through an audio device, without having to translate from third to second person as he reads.

The objectives are the most fundamental component of the Learning Model. Because this is a student lesson plan, the objectives should be couched in the same language as would be used in one-to-one confrontation with the student for whom it was designed. Proficiency, time and quantity specifications can be added at a later date for PPBS purposes, but to do so during the curriculum production phase not only is a waste of teacher time, but also is meaningless to the student.

The number of objectives appropriate for any one concept can only be determined by visualizing a student performing the task outlined. If the teacher feels it is likely that a pupil could fully understand the concept while performing the task outlined in a single objective, then no more objectives are needed. However, if it is possible that such a task could be achieved in the absence of full understanding, then the gap must be covered by one or more additional objectives. Another important consideration, of course, involves writing objectives at the higher levels of the cognitive taxonomy.

At this point, the pupil is encouraged to conduct a self-analysis of his ability in comparison with the objectives stated. If he thinks he can already perform as described, he is encouraged to take the PRETEST. If he is successful in the pretest, he may skip completely the learning activities and move into an activity of his own choosing which may or may not be related to the objectives. This type of independent movement through the curriculum is motivational both to the student and to his peer group. The student may be allowed to grade and log his own pretest or it may be administered by a teacher or aide.

The LEARNING ACTIVITIES should be as diversified as possible to allow for a wide variety of ways that a concept might be learned or that the objectives might be achieved. Many students have been known to study the learning activities section prior to asking for a pretest in order to make the teacher think that they could achieve the objectives all along. In reality, the student became a self-directed learner while attempting to be a "con artist." Such open and free use of the learning activities is what encourages the self-analysis, self-assessment, self-direction and self-diagnosis that tends to turn learning into a "fun thing to do" for students.

An interesting but vital sidelight to the learning activities section is that this is where the accountability finger can be turned to point at others rather than at only the teacher. In this section the lack of educational support glares from the dark recesses of the empty classroom media cabinet. As we trace the Learning Model from CONCEPT to OBJECTIVES to LEARNING ACTIVI-TIES, we are going from what students are to learn, to what they are to do as evidence of learning, to what route they can go in learning to perform the objectives. Just because we may reach agreement between educators and taxpayers concerning the first two components does not mean that the objectives will be achieved. If the only resources for learning are (1) the teacher explaining a given concept, and (2) the child reading page 39 of the basic text (and if the child doesn't read, 50 percent of that meager list is gone), then we who are the taxpaying public have failed to assume our share of the accountability charge. Therefore, in the learning activities section, teachers are encouraged to list media and materials that are on the market that they know might help some students achieve the objective, even though particular items may not yet be available in their school. To list media that are referenced to learning objectives is compatible with the intent of PPBS and provides the teacher with an automatic ready-reference budget request, supported with behavioral objectives.

The POSTTEST should be identical to the pretest, or enough like it to allow for accurate growth measurement. The posttest should be administered under the direction of the teacher.

The list of QUEST suggestions is the final section of the Learning Model. It is designed with the highly motivated, rapid learner in mind. Quest must not be an extension of the learning activities phase. For older children, it should not even contain suggestions. It is important that the student do his personal "thing" during the quest phase. If a quest suggestion can double as a learning activity for acquiring the concept or objective, then it is not an appropriate quest suggestion.

Summary

The Learning Model should be limited to one page. The reason for this suggestion is to insure that the package and the total curriculum retain flexibility. By binding the packages from a given curricular area in a notebook, for example, the packages for several grade levels can be of easy access to all. They contain the same essential data as the old learning activity packages but do not require the many file cabinets for such material. Flexibility is also realized in the simplicity of the Learning Model. Changes, additions and deletions are encouraged as the packages are used, thereby helping keep them constantly up to date. Gone is the tedious work necessary to update the multi-paged package format.

Utilizing graduate course offerings at no cost to the school district, the Alhambra City Schools have completed a continuous progress performance curriculum for all concepts in the language arts and mathematics, grades K-8. It is the experience of the Alhambra teachers that this type of learning package truly encourages individualized instruction, team teaching, flexible scheduling and performance reporting to parents. Additionally, those teachers who have been involved in the preparation phase have proven to be the ones who make the best use of the resulting curricular packages.

Leonard F. Dalton is Director of Curriculum, Alhambra (California) City Schools, and President, Unipac Inc., Glendora, California.

The Learning Activity Package (LAP)

James E. Smith, Jr.

What are we in today's elementary and secondary schools really trying to assist students to be able to do or be? Stated differently, what are the goals in education today? Once goals are established and agreed upon, *then*, and *only* then can we organize to meet them.

The reader may agree with all or merely some of the goals listed below. The important point is that school personnel need to have goals for their students and then organize the curriculum (content) and instruction (teaching-learning strategies) to permit each student to best reach these goals.

The following goals are all obtainable. They are applicable to individual students working in each classroom. You are encouraged to closely scrutinize them and see if they fit into what you are trying to do to assist the students with whom you work.

Goal No. 1: Help each student to increase his achievement level in the content areas of language, social studies, mathematics, science, art and music.

Goal No. 2: Help each student to develop the ability to direct his own learning. Specifically, assist a student to learn how to learn.

Goal No. 3: Help each student to develop a positive self-concept. Specifically, each student should possess realistic confidence in himself.

Goal No. 4: Help each student to assume increasing amounts of social responsibility.

Goal No. 5: Help each student to acquire, prior to his leaving formal schooling, a saleable skill.

Individualized instruction is not a goal. It is a way of organizing that permits and encourages each student to progress at a pace and level and in a manner commensurate with his unique combination of abilities, previous achievement, cultural background, interests, learning style and needs. Individualized instruction on the surface may seem rather simple and straightforward. On the contrary, it is complex and requires the consideration of several variables at the same time. Some of these variables are the following:

Content—Is it continuous, appropriate and relevant?

Staff—Can all those working with students (both professional and non-professional) be organized to take advantage of the strengths of each?

Schedule—Can students, space, staff, equipment and materials be brought together at the right moment for each student?

Facilities—Can space be so designed as to be appropriate to the activity involved, accessible to students and readily used for different purposes?

Self-Instructional Units (Learning Activity Packages)—Can materials be developed from which students can receive many of their directions, freeing the teacher to work with individuals and small groups?

Classroom Organization—Can systems be developed that permit each student to receive individual diagnoses and prescription; to better utilize the furniture, equipment and materials in the classroom so each student can work on his own or in small groups; to keep track of individual student progress; to report student progress to parents, etc.?

In summary, we need broad, agreed-upon goals. Individualizing instruction is a way of organizing to meet these goals. And finally, there are several variables, including self-instructional materials, that must be coordinated if we are going to individualize instruction.

The LAP

LAP Definition. A "Learning Activity Package" is a form of communication between the student and the teacher that contains instructions for student activities leading toward specified performance outcomes. The Activity Package is designed to individualize instruction consistent with the factors in the definition of "individualized instruction" given above.

LAP Components. The initial consideration in the preparation of any type of self-instructional learning module must be the organization of the body of content to be presented. The content can be drawn from a conceptual framework, or from an organizational pattern dictated by a highly specialized process. In any case, the organization should be immediately and clearly communicated to the learner.

The *TITLE* of the Activity Package should reflect the central theme, or *primary idea*, of the unit of work. Depending upon the amount or magnitude of the body of content, this primary idea may be broken down into *secondary ideas* (three to five subdivisions or constituent parts of the larger primary idea).

Once this decision has been reached, the *RATIONALE,* a narrative statement to the student, should be prepared. This statement should communicate to the learner the overall intent of the package and its importance or relevance to the student's course of study. It should be clear and concise, and should lend continuity to previous and subsequent learning experiences.

Much content is dependent upon previous learning, i.e., it is placed somewhere on a continuum or spiral of learning experience. If this is the case, a short *PREREQUISITE KNOWLEDGE SELF-ASSESSMENT INSTRUMENT* should be included. This should indicate to both learner and teacher whether the student possesses the prerequisite information (knowledge, skills, etc.) for probable success with the Activity Package.

The most fundamental component for guiding or structuring the behavior of the learner is a set of *OBJECTIVES.* These objectives should be behaviorally stated and should specify the intent, performance conditions and the minimum acceptable level of performance. Diversity in levels of learning sophistication (i.e., recall, application, synthesis) should be provided so that the student is directed toward higher-level thought processes rather than confined to mere recall and regurgitation of factual information. The domain (whether it be cognitive, affective or psychomotor), the number of objectives and the levels of performance are all considerations which are dictated by the content and the manner in which the content is organized.

Once the intent and the specific performance criteria (*objectives*) of the Activity Package have been communicated to the learner, a *SELF-EVALUATION* should be provided. This form of evaluation may be student- or teacher-directed but it should serve the following purposes:

1. allow the student to bypass the Activity Package if he can already meet the performance criteria;
2. guide the student to those portions of the Activity Package that he needs to study; and,
3. allow the student to check on his own progress level prior to the *TEACHER EVALUATION*.

Special note should be taken that evaluations need not be exclusively paper-and-pencil types. They can be product oriented, group discussion oriented, or manipulative performance oriented.

Some Activity Packages may require two additional components: a set of *SPECIAL STUDENT DIRECTIONS* and/or a set of *GENERAL CLASSROOM MANAGEMENT PROCEDURES*. The necessity for including student directions is dependent upon the content to be presented, the organization of the material, the use of specialized equipment or facilities and the implications for time or scheduling of activities. The inclusion of classroom management procedures is appropriate if it is necessary to state, for example, the location to which a student should submit completed papers of projects, or directions for finding certain types of resource materials and equipment, etc.

The "heart" or core of the Activity Package is the *LEARNING ACTIVITIES* component. These activities should provide each student with a choice of alternatives concerning not only how, what, when and where to learn but also opportunities for the efficient use of a wide range of learning resources. Stated another way, these activities should provide the learner with alternatives in terms of the following:

1. *Multi-media*—the use of various kinds of audio-visual equipment and the performance of sensory-oriented tasks;

2. *Multi-mode*—variations in process goals that determine the size of the learning group and the methodology (i.e., large-group instruction, small-group instruction, individual work);

3. *Multi-content*—differing levels of sophistication or difficulty of all resource materials, whether printed or audio-visual; and,

4. *Multi-activities*—variations in terms of paper-and-pencil activities, such as listening, viewing, speaking, participating in academic games and simulations, manipulating, etc.

It should be noted here that congruence between PRETEST, OBJECTIVES, ACTIVITIES, and POSTTEST (terminal TEACHER EVALUATION) must be built into any package. In other words, you must (1) specify the level and conditions of acceptable performance, (2) provide learning activities incorporating the "multis" which relate to these objectives and which permit in-depth or further work, and (3) ensure that all forms of assessment or evaluation, at the stated level and under the stated conditions, measure that which you indicated would be measured.

The final component of the Learning Activity Package may be classified as an addendum: the *TEACHER'S INSTRUCTIONS* section. This section should include that information which is extraneous to the student package but which is, nevertheless, essential to the smooth presentation, management and evaluation of the system. The discipline and level should be clearly stated. If an unusual organizational approach has been utilized, it should be clearly defined and explained. If the content of the Activity Package is dependent upon previous learning, the conditions, objectives and procedures for using the *PREREQUISITE SELF-ASSESSMENT* should be clearly delineated. A vitally important component for teachers who are using an Activity Package prepared by someone else is a detailed and coded bibliography of resources. Notes or suggestions to the teacher in terms of methodological approaches or strengths, or other special instructions, should be included and, perhaps, a list of professional sources of information. Finally, the *TEACHER EVALUATION* should be included in this section. The nature, length and conditions of this posttest will, of course, be dictated by the objectives. This instrument should provide equivalent conditions to those stated in the objectives.

Package Structure and Design

Once the content around which the package is going to be constructed has been decided upon and each of the components has been developed, the question arises as to how to make the LAP easy to use and attractive. Several techniques have been used to answer this question. What is *not* desired is a booklet that resembles the bibliography frequently given to students at the initial meeting of a college course, namely, four pages of single-spaced reference sources. What *is* desired is the following:

1. *Attractive use of space*: Too much print on any one page tends to discourage the user.
2. *Use of color*: The LAP can be made quite functional and more attractive by color coding the various sections.
3. *Use of illustrations*: Through cartoon characters and other forms of illustrations, content messages can be conveyed and/or motivation can be enhanced.
4. *Use of "tying together" type of messages*: Between the various components, messages to students add continuity to the LAP. An example would be a message between the objectives and pretest, such as "You have just read the objectives. If you feel you can already meet all or some of the objectives or would merely like to find out for yourself what you do or do not know, try the pretest on the next page. The answers to the pretest can be found on page 8."
5. *Use of small boxes or circles in front of each learning activity statement*: The teacher and student can, by

placing the date assigned, due date and date completed in these boxes, or circles, help add structure to a seemingly unstructured situation.

6. *Placing of contracts in the LAP where students can, after a conference with the teacher or on their own, agree to complete a segment or the entire LAP by a certain time:* Again the purpose here is to provide structure to those students requiring structure.

Writing LAPs

It is the author's opinion that, up to this point, a standardized LAP (that is, a LAP that can be used by teachers throughout the country or even in two neighboring school districts) has not been developed. Perhaps it is because of a lack of common agreement on the part of teachers as to what content should be taught or what objectives are really important, or the lack of common learning resources in different districts, or some other reason not mentioned.

No matter what the causes of this dilemma, it is suggested that the staff within a school or district write their own LAPs. The steps many have used in proceeding to do this are the following:

1. A process-oriented workshop should be conducted, helping all professional staff members develop one complete LAP. It is suggested that this process be individualized to model for the staff how they in turn might work best with their students.
2. Teachers who are most effective and efficient in writing LAPs should be identified from those participating in the workshop.
3. A plan should be developed that schedules the development of LAPs over a two- to four-year period, involving teachers who wish to do this kind of work and who have been identified as being efficient and effective.
4. All teachers in a district should be involved in identifying content, objectives and learning activities; in critiquing the packages before they are used; in using the packages; and in providing feedback for revising.

Summary

The first section of this paper dealt with placing the LAP into perspective. It is imperative that LAPs or individualizing instructions not be made paramount, but merely that they be thought of as tools and systems to better meet goals.

The second section dealt with the definition of the LAP, the components that make up this type of package, ways of designing the LAP so as to make it functional and attractive, and systematic methods for accomplishing the job of LAP writing at the district level.

It should be kept in mind that the LAP is the reflection of an attitude towards students and will, when written, do only that which the writer allows it to do—no more and no less.

James E. Smith, Jr., is President, Educational Associates, Inc., Fort Lauderdale, Florida.

The PLAN System
as an Application
of Educational Technology

John C. Flanagan

Technology has two kinds of applications which can be of important assistance in improving education. The first of these is comprised of various hardware developments. These include the computer, audio and video tapes, slides, filmstrips, motion pictures and television. The latter includes not only the commercial and educational broadcasts but closed circuit and the new cassette-type presentations. New equipment is becoming available which will make possible types of classroom assistance which have not been possible heretofore. The second type of assistance technology can give to education is the use of sophisticated methodological procedures such as the systems approach to problem solution. In general, effective applications of technology start with a clearly defined problem rather than with looking for ways in which a new piece of equipment can be used.

In the field of education, the problems and deficiencies of the nation's schools have been frequently reported. One of the most comprehensive and dramatic of these reports resulted from the 1960 Project TALENT survey. Using the criterion for acceptable comprehension of paragraphs as the giving of correct answers to at least half of the questions on the ideas expressed in this paragraph, it was found that less than half of the twelfth grade students in a representative national sample achieved this level of comprehension for typical paragraphs taken from the *Readers Digest.* Similarly, only twenty-five percent of the high school seniors achieved this degree of comprehension of typical paragraphs taken from *Time Magazine,* and only four percent of the twelfth grade students achieved this level of comprehension for typical paragraphs selected from the *Saturday Review.*

An indication of the inappropriateness of learning experiences provided for many students was shown in the answer to the questions regarding study habits. For example, about forty percent of the students reported that "Half the time, or more frequently, I seem to accomplish very little compared to the amount of time I spend studying." Similarly, about forty-five percent of the twelfth grade students sampled said that "Lack of interest in my school work makes it difficult for me to keep my attention on what I am doing." This lack of interest and attention was experienced half the time or more. An update of this national survey in 1970 indicated very similar results.

Another important deficiency in education which was revealed by the 1960 Project TALENT survey was the lack of purposefulness and goals among the students in secondary schools. In the original survey, only a relatively small number of the boys and girls reported that they were "very definite" or "completely decided" in their choice of an occupation. In the 1970 update, slightly less of them—25.5 percent of the eleventh graders— indicated one of these choices. This lack of clear goals is also shown in the instability of the career choices among high school students. Only 18.6 percent of the twelfth grade boys and 26.1 percent of the twelfth grade girls planned the same career five years after finishing high school that they were planning when in the twelfth grade.

The other deficiency in American education which was emphasized by the findings from this study was the serious failure to make any adequate allowance for individual differences. For example, it was discovered that twenty-five to thirty percent of the ninth grade students already knew more about English and social studies than did the average twelfth grader. Nevertheless, most of these ninth graders were being collected in classes of twenty-five or thirty and given identical instruction within these classes. Many students were being asked to learn things that were practically impossible for them to understand from the materials presented while others were wasting time on materials they already knew.

Goals and Strategies of the PLAN System

On the basis of the deficiencies and problems in American Education as exemplified by the findings from Project TALENT quoted above, it was proposed that four basic concepts characterize the proposed solution to these problems.

1. *The development of each individual student should be the goal of the educational system.* Many recent efforts to improve education have been focused on teaching methods, audio-visual equipment, teaching machines and computers. The PLAN system (Program for Learning in Accordance with Needs) has chosen to focus on the individual and his needs for educational development.

2. *To achieve the development of each individual student, a comprehensive survey of a wide variety of learning methods and materials should be studied, and those most appropriate selected for the learning of each of the student's objectives.* This concept will be recognized as one of the important steps in applying the systems approach to a problem. Once the objectives have been established, a variety of alternate procedures for obtaining them should be compared.

3. *An effective educational system can be most efficiently developed by a team consisting of teachers, administrators, scholars and curriculum experts, assisted by a group of measurement, research and evaluation experts.* Many efforts to improve education have failed because of the reliance on one or two of these groups to carry the whole burden. The experience and judgment of classroom teachers regarding the learning habits, interests and characteristics of students are essential. However, most teachers lack the necessary expertise in both curriculum development and measurement and evaluation to implement a new system of education without assistance.

4. *To insure both the individual development of the student and the development and the improvement of the system, it is essential to have a program of continuous evaluation with respect to all of the objectives on which the students are engaged.* To make it possible for the student to move on to the next objective as soon as he has mastered one, measuring instruments must be available, and both the student and the teacher need to be

informed as to whether or not he has mastered the specific objectives covered by a set of learning materials. Similarly, the accumulation of information regarding performance of students after using particular learning methods and materials can provide a basis for improving the selection of learning procedures for later students. Finally, it is essential to evaluate the progress of each student with respect to the plans for his educational development.

The Development and Operation of the PLAN
Educational System

The PLAN educational system was developed over a four-year period from about 1966 to 1970. An initial decision was that a modular program would be developed so that each student could learn the facts and principles and acquire the abilities and appreciations most important to his individual development. The program was designed to include learning modules in four areas: mathematics, science, language arts and social studies. For each of these it was proposed that learning modules be developed from grade one through grade twelve. To assist in the planning of the coverage of each of these four areas, national curriculum advisory panels were appointed. These included (1) for mathematics: Howard Fehr, Columbia University Teachers College; Donovan Johnson, University of Minnesota; Burt Kaufman, Southern Illinois University; and Hans Zassenhaus, Ohio State University; (2) for science: Robert Gagne, Florida State University; Paul DeHart Hurd, Stanford University; and Robert Karplus, University of California, Berkeley; (3) for language arts: Francis Christensen, University of Southern California; Julius Hook, University of Illinois; Walter Loban, University of California, Berkeley; Robert Ruddell, University of California, Berkeley; and Ruth Strickland, University of Illinois; and (4) for social studies: Richard Gross, Stanford University; John Haefner, University of Iowa; John Michaelis, University of California, Berkeley; and Roy Price, Syracuse University. These advisory panels worked with subject matter specialists on the staff of the American Institutes for Research in selecting the topics and outlining their scope and sequence for the twelve levels. In planning the work in each of these fields, many more modules were included than any one student would be expected to complete. Thus, it was intended that each student be assisted in selecting those modules most appropriate for his individual program of studies.

In dividing the content and skills into modules it was planned that each module require an average of about two weeks for mastery by the typical student. To provide more precise reports to the student and teacher as to the content and skills which were mastered, each module was made up of about five specific objectives. The decision as to the level of specificity/generality for objectives is a critical one. In some cases teachers have listed several thousand objectives for a one-semester course. This degree of specificity is self-defeating because the volume of record keeping is likely to smother the whole system. With a two-week module it was anticipated that each student would complete something less than twenty modules during a year. With about five objectives for each module, this means that there would be about one hundred specific objectives that he would master during the year.

The mastery of each objective is measured by a test, usually consisting of five to ten items. Thus a module test which measures separately the mastery of each of five objectives ordinarily includes between twenty-five and fifty test items.

To assist the student in learning the objectives for a module, a student guide, which is called a teaching-learning unit, is prepared. These guides were prepared by teachers from the schools participating in the development of PLAN. A teaching-learning unit consists of four parts for each objective. First is the statement of the objective in terms of the type of performance a student should be able to demonstrate if he has mastered the objective. The second part is a specific test item to illustrate the specific type of achievement expected. The third portion of the teaching-learning unit directs the student to a specific textbook, workbook, tape or other learning material which he is to use to master the objective. The fourth part contains detailed specifications of what the student should do with these learning materials to master the specific objective. The other essential component of each module, in addition to the teaching-learning unit, is the module test. The test items for each objective are prepared by specialists on the project staff.

Thus the essential parts of the PLAN instructional system include a set of objectives, arranged in modules, covering a specific scope and sequence of materials; a group of teaching-learning units designed to assist the student in achieving these objectives; and last, a set of module tests designed to measure each objective in the module to determine whether or not the student has mastered this particular objective.

These are the essential parts of this type of an instructional system. Of course, with this sort of system, an indefinite number of teaching-learning units can be developed using specific textbooks, workbooks and other materials to master the specific objectives of the module. The objectives and tests would remain fixed, but the alternate procedures for achieving mastery of these objectives could be very large. In an effective and sophisticated system, it would be expected that over a period of time the inefficient procedures would be eliminated and, insofar as possible, each student would be provided a teaching-learning unit which would direct him to those learning experiences which would be of greatest interest to him and which would best match his style of learning.

Support Components for the PLAN System

For this type of individualized instructional system to be effective, three other components are necessary. The first of these components is a guidance program which will assist each student in planning his long-range goals and educational objectives. Such a program can provide the basis for developing a program of studies for each student which will make it possible to achieve individual goals. The second component is a program for teacher development which will assist the teacher in adapting to the new teaching role required by the PLAN educational system. The third component is the computer support system which performs a number of functions including test scoring and reporting, record keeping, the development of periodic summary reports of progress and the development of sophisticated programs of studies for students. Such programs of studies are based on all of the information available regarding the interests and present status of the students with respect to the abilities, facts and principles necessary to achieve their objectives. These components are especially important because they go beyond how the student learns or whether he has learned. They accomplish the very important functions of determining what is most appropriate for the student to learn and of providing the support and assistance to enable him to master these specified objectives and attain his goals.

The Plan Guidance System. It is obviously of critical importance that the student learn those things necessary for his individual development. When schools changed their focus from educating an elite to educating all the children, inadequate provision was made for assisting students with the necessary decisions and choices. Assisting a student to formulate goals and plans is an essential function of the PLAN program. An effort has been made, as with the instructional system, to utilize available materials where possible. However, in the guidance field much of the program had to be developed because of the lack of suitable materials in this area. The five functions of this program are described briefly below.

1. The first function is to acquaint the student with the varieties of opportunities, roles and activities available in the field of occupations and in personal, social and civic relations. The materials and procedures for performing this function were developed under the direction of James A. Dunn of the staff of the American Institutes for Research. To accomplish this, a series of modules was embedded in the social studies program throughout all levels of instruction. In the primary grades the objectives emphasize the nature of work, interaction between persons in various jobs, work as a means of making a living and as a means of obtaining personal satisfactions, the functions occupations perform with respect to economic needs, and the ways in which people prepare for occupations.

In the intermediate grades the modules introduce the concept of job families, acquaint the student with the kinds of occupations included in each job family, discuss trends in the occupations field, and give the student detailed information regarding about fifty of the currently important occupations. At the secondary level this study of specific occupations within the basic job families is continued. The educational requirements for specific careers and the levels of achievement in terms of developed abilities required by each of these occupations are made available.

2. The performance of the second function, the student's formulation of his own goals and plans, requires that the student know not only about occupations and their requirements but about the status of his own development with respect to abilities, interests, physical and social characteristics, and values. In addition to giving the student an opportunity to take tests that will provide an estimate of his present developed abilities to perform various types of functions and his interests and preferences, it is important that the student gain an understanding of the nature of individual differences and the basic principles underlying learning activities which might enable him to attain certain required levels of performance with respect to specific abilities.

A twelve-scale PLAN interest inventory and an eighteen-part Developed Abilities Performance Test were developed to enable the student to compare his interests and ability levels with those of people who later entered various occupations. On the basis of his results from these tests, each student can determine whether he has developed his abilities to the required levels for obtaining advanced training for various careers in which he might be interested. He can also verify his expressed interests in various types of occupations and estimate the extent of effort required to develop his abilities to meet the entrance requirements if he has not already attained this level.

3. The third function, the formulation of the individual's long-range goals and the development of plans for their attainment, is probably the most important step required of him during his educational years. To perform these tasks effectively, the student needs not only information about himself in relation to the requirements of various occupations but also skill in problem-

solving and decision-making. There is no single answer to the most appropriate occupation for an individual, and the student must learn to weigh his values and the potential satisfactions from a particular choice with the effort which will be required to attain that particular goal.

4. The fourth function represents an important aspect of the guidance program on which only limited progress has been made. This is to assist the student in acquiring competence in managing his own development. The intent is to assist the student to learn to carry out a personal program involving the selective reinforcement of desirable behaviors which will enable him to attain his goals.

5. The final function of the guidance program relates to assisting the student in making a smooth transition from high school to the occupational field or to advanced educational opportunities and to the responsibilities of citizenship.

The Teacher Development Program. The fact that the PLAN educational system represents an individualized approach to education does not mean that the teacher does not have a critical role. The traditional types of teacher training do not prepare the teacher, however, for the specific activities essential for effective assistance to students in the PLAN program. Teacher development in PLAN consists of four phases: first is a phase in which the teacher visits PLAN classes being conducted by experienced teachers to observe the program in action and get a feel for the role of the teacher in this situation. This is ordinarily done in the spring of the year prior to the teacher's entry into the PLAN educational program. The second phase is a reading period in which articles and handbooks discussing the basic concepts and philosophy underlying PLAN and individualized education in general are reviewed and reacted to. The third phase consists of three or four days during which an individualized program using modules, teaching-learning units, objectives and tests modeled after the PLAN system are provided the teacher. These modules are designed to acquaint the teacher with the basic information and skills essential for conducting a class in the PLAN system. After the teacher has begun her work with a PLAN class, a supervisor observes the teacher and checks on mastery of specific skills important for the effective functioning of PLAN. The results of these checks are discussed with the teacher, and together they develop a program to remedy any defects observed.

The Role of the Computer. The computer performs three principal functions in the PLAN educational system. These include daily processing, management information and the development of a program of studies for the individual student. The work described as daily processing includes a number of functions related to classroom management. When the student completes the work for a module, as described in the particular teaching-learning unit which he received, he takes the module test by recording his answers to the questions on an optical-scan-type card used in connection with the card reader in the school building (currently an IBM 2956). These cards contain the responses for twenty-seven five-choice items. Where more than this number of items are required a second card is used. Other cards used with the terminal include a registration card, a student status card, a teacher action card, an observation and comments card and a teacher supplies card. The teacher may transmit these cards at intervals throughout the day. All processing is done by the central computer, usually at a remote location and returned during the night so that the results are available to the teacher in the morning. The computer scores the various tests submitted and responds to other messages transmitted on the special cards included. These data are transmitted over telephone lines to the automatic typewriter (IBM 2740) which is part of the PLAN terminal in the school building.

The teacher print-out ordinarily includes four sections. The first section is an exception section, noting additional information needed for specific cards which were transmitted. The second section acknowledges various teacher actions. The third section is a planning section. The fourth is a test results section. This is usually the main section of the report. For each of the objectives in a particular module there is a specific report on the number correct in relation to the total number of items measuring this objective. A message accompanying these results indicates whether the student is ready to go on to the next module or needs to review materials related to one or more of the objectives before proceeding to the next module.

The second function of the computer relates to the management aspects of both the student's progress and the quality of the system. Periodically the computer will print out the progress each student has made with respect to his program of studies. This enables the principal or other supervisor to know exactly the status of each class and each student with respect to the program. The other type of periodic report prepared includes item analysis for those groups of students who have taken a particular module test after using a specified teaching-learning unit to prepare for this test. The computer also keeps a record of how much time was spent by the student on each module. These types of management information make it possible to assist the teacher in insuring satisfactory progress from each student and also make it possible to improve the operation of the system.

The third function of the computer is to prepare a program of studies for each student. This is ordinarily done annually, but the program of studies might be updated at any time on the basis of new information. The computer program makes use of all of the information available about the student. The first type of information consists of his placement along the scale of required modules in the particular subject. In determining this placement, his performance on the objectives included in the module tests is checked against performance on periodic achievement tests which include a sample of items measuring the various objectives which the student has completed. The second type of information required to develop the program of studies is to determine a quota in terms of the specific number of modules the student is expected to complete during the year. Usually this is based on two types of data: first, the number of modules completed during the previous year and second, a weighted combination of the scores of the student on the Developed Ability Performance Tests. The weights are determined for each subject in each grade on the basis of the best prediction of the number of modules completed by students in that grade during the previous year.

The most complicated step in the development of the program of studies involves the selection of the specific modules to be included in the student's program of studies. This selection is based on the state and local requirements in this subject matter field, the occupational family that the student and parent have selected as his long-range goal after comparing his scores on the interest test and Developed Ability Performance tests with scores made by persons entering these fields, and the computer-suggested long-range goal based on all the information available. Whenever it seems possible, students and teachers are given options to permit the student to explore current interests, but at the same time insure that he is achieving the basic concepts and principles essential for further development in the field. These programs of study are based directly on data obtained from and about the student and the information available in the records from the previous year. However, the student and teacher are free at any time to modify the initial program of studies on the basis of new information or special circumstances. Such a program of study permits much greater flexibility in terms of the specific aspects of a course which a student needs to prepare for his future activities and roles.

Conclusion

Certainly the current trend towards accountability in education requires the kind of detailed documentation of progress and also the kind of assurance that relevant educational experiences are being provided that are basic to the PLAN educational system. Perhaps the most important aspect of PLAN is the turning over of responsibility to each student for his own educational development. It would, of course, be indefensible to do this without preparing the student to take this responsibility. Early indications are that the system has been effective in assisting students to accept responsibility for their own educational development.

The PLAN educational system, being distributed by Westinghouse Learning Corporation, was used by approximately 30,000 students in various school districts throughout the country during the 1971-72 year. The PLAN system is designed as a tool in the development of an educational program which is effective, relevant and accountable for today's students.

John C. Flanagan is President, American Institutes for Research, Palo Alto, California.

The Duluth Contract:
What It Is and What It Does

Thorwald Esbensen

Following is an example of a Duluth Student Learning Contract:

Content Classification
Creative writing—using familiar words in unfamiliar ways.

Purpose
In school, when you are assigned to write something, do you sometimes feel that you don't know how to make what you have to say sound interesting? Many people (not just students) seem to have trouble making words come alive. There is no answer to this problem, of course. But there are some simple things you can do to get more life into what you write. The purpose of this contract is to give you practice in using ordinary words in unusual ways, and to do so in a manner that will be fun for you and any of your classmates who choose this work.

Performance Objective
Given the task of describing an object, person, or event, the student will be able to do so using words ordinarily reserved for a different kind of object, person, or event (e.g., describing an inanimate object as though it were animate).

Evaluation
In not more than fifty words (using any form of prose or poetry) do one of the following:
- describe a clock as a villain
- describe a truck convoy as animals at night
- describe a woman as a bird or an insect
- describe the sun as an orchestra leader
- describe the moon as a trapeze performer
- describe a group of mountains as a family
- describe the wind as an artist

Taxonomy Category
   Invention

Resources
   (1) *The Word Weaver,* by Barbara Esbensen
   (2) Excerpt from *Legendary Masters of the Piano*
   (3) *Honey and Salt,* by Carl Sandburg
   (4) *Swing Around the Sun,* by Barbara Esbensen
   (5) Poetry by Emily Dickinson
   (6) Teacher-led presentation
   (7) Etc.

Certain things about this contract should be noted. First, it is brief, not more than one page in length. The reason for this is that teachers (for the most part) must write contracts. And teachers have little enough time as it is to do the many things they have to do. Thus something relatively short and simple is desirable.

Second, it is designed to be a miniature lesson plan for direct use by individual students. This means that its six parts (Content Classification, Purpose, Performance Objective, Evaluation, Taxonomy Category, Resources) are designed to include all the information that would be needed by a student working on his own within a program of individualized instruction. (When Contracts are used with students who are not able to read them, kindergarteners or first graders, for example, the contents of the Contracts must be communicated in other ways. The teacher might do this personally, or other students might help. Prerecorded tapes or pictures are additional possibilities.)

Let us look at each of the six parts of the Contract in terms of the sample Contract given above.

Content Classification
Content Classification simply states where in a subject matter outline or curriculum guide a particular Contract fits. This is a familiar notion to educators.

Purpose
The Purpose paragraph answers the question "Why?" It

attempts to say why the Contract deserves a place in the overall scheme of instruction. Of what value is it? Why is it worth a student's attention? Once again, teachers are used to addressing themselves to this sort of task.

Performance Objective

The Performance Objective is a description of what can stand as evidence that something has been accomplished. It explains in terms of observable student performance what it is that a student must be able to do in order to show that he has mastered the Contract. Once a student has familiarized himself with the use of Contracts, the performance objective is the first thing he usually looks at when he receives a new Contract.

Evaluation

The Evaluation item illustrates how the student's accomplishment of the performance objective will be tested, how he will be checked out on his Contract. Often, a sample situation is described so that the student, by means of a specific example, can have a clear idea of exactly how his mastery of the contract will be determined.

Taxonomy Category

The Duluth contract system uses a simplified form of the Bloom *Taxonomy of Educational Objectives.* Its purpose is simply to provide teachers (and interested others) with an opportunity to look at their whole range of contracts in order to see whether most of them are up on top of the water, so to speak, requiring only recall or recognition, or whether there is a wider spread of learning skills being called for.

Resources

A list of learning resources is the final part of the Contract. Here are listed the various materials, activities and persons that are available to the student in order to help him master the Contract. It is not necessary for the student to work through all of the items listed under resources. He need use only those items that are

necessary to his achievement of the Contract objective. This means
that, in rare instances, a student may decide that he is ready to be
evaluated before he has employed any of the designated resources.
This is fair. Demonstrated accomplishment rather than time served
or resources used is the criterion of successful achievement.

How large should the performance objective of a contract be?
On the one hand, it should be small enough so that a student may
have assurance of success within a relatively short period of time.
On the other hand, it should be large enough so that the teacher
does not have to spend most of his time checking students in and
out of Contracts. This means that the feasible size of Contracts
will depend in part upon the efficiency of information recording
and retrieving systems, as well as the use of teacher aides, student
self-checking arrangements, etc. At the present time, most
Contracts seem to be written so that the mythical average student
can complete one or two contracts per week in a given subject.

Applications of the
Contract Approach

The contract approach to instruction is applicable to a
variety of situations. One possibility involves the four-fold use of
student Contracts. Under this arrangement, the student may work
with Contracts in four different ways.

Alternative One is the *teacher-made* and *teacher-assigned*
Contract. That is to say, the student has little or no choice in what
he is to learn. This seems to be the most prevalent form of
Contract usage at the present time. *Prescriptive* approaches to
instruction generally appear to favor this mode of operation.

Alternative Two is the *teacher-made* but *student-assigned*
Contract. From the bank of Contracts which the teacher has
created (or organized) and selected for the student, the learner
may choose which one he will work on next. This alternative calls
into question some of the traditional assumptions concerning
scope and sequence. It challenges the idea that in such matters the
teacher always knows best.

Alternative Three is the *student-made* and *student-assigned*
Contract in an area that the student has identified as being a

weakness for himself. This alternative encourages the learner to engage in some self-prescription. It prompts him to do some thinking about himself for himself.

Alternative Four promotes another kind of self-prescription. It uses the *student-made* and *student-assigned* Contract in an area that the student has identified as being of *special interest* to himself. This alternative runs *counter* to the practice of emphasizing to students what it is they *don't* know, what they *lack*, what is *wrong* with them. It attempts to build on student strengths and interests. It rejects the flat achievement profile as an ideal and opts for personal preferences instead.

A particularly exciting use of student Contracts began in 1971-72 at the West End School of St. Jean's parish in Duluth, Minnesota. The entire school staff, grades one through eight, is making it possible for each family individually to decide what its children shall learn in school. The curricular offerings are in the form of Contracts organized into curriculum catalogs. Each family has a complete set of catalogs and, through a series of individual school and family conferences held throughout the year, is able to choose the specific Contracts that a given child will attempt to accomplish over a designated period of time (usually six weeks). This project, in other words, sees educational accountability resting, in the final analysis, on the base of customer satisfaction. It says, in effect, that in a democratic society every family has the inalienable right to make its own mistakes. It does not need the school to mandate what must be learned on the basis of that institution's demonstrated fallibility in such matters.

Questions concerning the St. Jean's family decision-making approach to individualized instruction may be directed to the writer at the College of St. Scholastica, Duluth, Minnesota.

Thorwald Esbensen is on the staff of the College of St. Scholastica, Duluth, Minnesota.

Materials for Individualized Instruction: An Interpretation of Goals

John O. Bolvin

A basic component of any instructional system consists of materials and resources available to the student to facilitate learning. However, educators' notions regarding the importance and role of materials in an instructional system are varied and at times even contradictory. In some instructional systems, materials are viewed as tools for the teacher and are often classified as "teaching aids," "aids for teachers" or "instructional aids." The implication here is that the teacher is the sole or at least the most prominent and important medium for the transmission of knowledge. In other systems, however, materials are referred to as "learning aids," "learning packs," etc., implying that the materials are for students and a key in the instructional process.

In the past, instructional materials have been looked upon more as tools for the teacher. Teachers would be provided with a core of materials, e.g., textbooks, filmstrips, workbooks, etc., and were then expected to modify, adapt and supplement these materials to better accommodate the needs of individual students. This concept seemed appropriate since the teacher was responsible for organizing the instructional process which met both the short- and long-range goals of the student being taught. Generally this cannot be considered a "bad" practice since most of us would agree that when provided the time, the skills and the resources, the best instructional materials for any student would be materials that are developed specifically to meet the needs of that particular student at a particular time.

The major problem with this is quite obvious. Teachers in the

48

conventional school setting can, at best, only develop materials to meet a few subgroups of students. These materials have to be of a type that can be generated easily and quickly in the time provided, as well as being inexpensive due to the quantities needed. What many educators fail to realize is that in this compromising situation where the teacher, or the teacher in combination with the student, is to develop the materials, we tend to identify materials that fit some generalized goals that may or may not fit the needs of individual students. This whole process runs counter to the basic purpose of materials in an individualized instructional system. Let us first examine some common goals for education, then a system designed to meet these goals and, finally, the role materials can play in reaching these goals.

Goals

A common theme that runs throughout the expression of educational goals is that we are attempting to develop an instructional system that can provide for the maximum individual fulfillment for each student within the schools. All of us can agree with the general goals as stated by Professor Jean Piaget:

The principal goal of education is to create men who are capable of doing new things, not simply of repeating what other generations have done—men who are creative, inventive and discoverers. The second goal of education is to form minds which can be critical, can verify, and not accept everything they are offered. The great danger today is of slogans, collective opinions, ready-made trends of thought. We have to be able to resist individually, to criticize, to distinguish between what is proven and what is not. So we need pupils who are active, who learn early to find out by themselves, partly by their own spontaneous activity and partly through materials we set up for them . . .[1]

One problem that arises when implementing such general goals is that they have little specific meaning for individual students within the educational system. Teachers are the first to realize that students within a classroom differ as to needs, interests and desires concerning their immediate goals with respect to the more general goals as just stated. However, teachers will also be the first to admit that they are given little help and have very few tools to assist in instructing the individual student relative to his more immediate goals and his position in realizing the long-range goals.

The question here, then, is how can we provide educational goals for students that make it possible for them to obtain the individual fulfillment as implied in the broad goals stated above? It appears that our solution to this problem in the past has been to establish a single set of goals for all students. As these students move from the elementary into the secondary level, four or five sets of goals are established for different groups of students (e.g., academic, commercial, vocational). In essence, this has moved educational institutions into the arena of screening instead of education. As students move through the program, those who are not able to satisfy the objectives at a given time are usually screened out either intentionally or unintentionally, thus closing the option of obtaining the broader goal that overrides the system. This screening process continues from the secondary schools into higher education (technical schools, colleges, universities) and into job possibilities. In general, this procedure for establishing goals is an over-simplification of goal setting and works to the disadvantage of many of the students coming through our public school system.

From what has been said thus far, it appears that a pressing need in education today is to adapt instructional materials to individual characteristics and background. This implies, first of all, a consideration of goals for the individual student within the educational system. This is not a new consideration or a new need; it has been the basis for most of the educational innovations in the past twenty years. However, it does seem now that society is becoming more committed to the significance of individual performance as opposed to group categorization. Education that is dedicated to being adaptive to individual needs must maximize individual competence and provide every individual with a sense of pride, uniqueness and a feeling of capability for participation as a full-fledged member in the development of our society.

The work of the Learning Research and Development Center (LRDC) at the University of Pittsburgh, as reflected in two of the projects, the Individually Prescribed Instruction Project and the Primary Education Project, represents an investigation into the requirements for and the problems encountered in developing a system to individualize instruction. The broad goals of our instructional system are not much different from those expressed previously in this article. We do agree with the goals of Professor Piaget, but as educational technologists, we are greatly concerned about the conditions and the educational environment which bring about such behaviors in the student.

Different definitions for individualized instruction can be proposed. The LRDC defines individualization as the adaptation of the educational environment to individual differences; or, putting it another way, individualized instruction is the development of an individual program of studies for each student based upon his learning needs and his characteristics as a learner. This definition assumes that educational goals are individual and that the student's plan must be in keeping with these goals. It is around this definition that the development and utilization of materials and resources within the instructional system are geared.

Objectives

The individual differences provided for in this system can probably be grouped into broad categories which include:[2]

(1) *Provisions for differences in level of achievement among pupils within a given class.* This means that the system is so structured that it is possible to determine what each child now knows in each of the curriculum areas as defined by the broad goals for the total school and what each child is ready to do to progress smoothly through the curriculum to his goals.

(2) *Provisions for the differences in rate of learning toward certain goals in the curriculum.* In order to provide for individual differences in rate of achieving these goals, it is necessary to restructure materials, techniques of instruction and the learning setting in an attempt to maximize each pupil's rate. For the

system to meet this need, it has to adapt to at least the gross learning styles of the student. Hopefully, one of the most important outcomes of the work at the LRDC will be the identification of the various learning styles among students in the same subject areas and within a particular student for different subject areas.

(3) *Provisions for establishing different learning goals for different students.* Even though most of the learning goals in the elementary school are common to most students, there are still those goals which can vary from student to student. This is particularly true as the student moves into the upper years of the elementary school. The determination of which goals to establish for which student at present is a joint decision between the child and the teacher depending upon the child's past experiences and achievement and his own long-range goals as they relate to the particular subject area.

The instructional system to meet these objectives can best be thought of in terms of the following components:

(1) *The outcomes of learning are specified in terms of observable competence and the conditions under which it is to be exercised.* In other words, a fundamental requirement in developing an individualized program is to first describe in terms of measurable products and assessable student performance the outcomes of instructional situations. If creativity, inquiry, complex reasoning and open-mindedness are desired aspects of human behaviors, then they should be recognized as accessible goals and specified as observable competencies.

(2) *Detailed diagnosis is made of the initial state in which a learner comes into a particular instructional situation.* Without careful assessment of initial learning characteristics, carrying out the educational procedure is a presumption. It is like prescribing medication for an illness without first describing the symptoms. The diagnosis of the initial state should include not only assessment of the learner's knowledge of prerequisite behaviors, but also the assessment of his aptitude, his learning style preferences and his perceptual and motor skill capabilities. This accumulative diagnosis or long-term history must be especially

relevant to the immediate instructional step that is to be taken. (3) *The immediate instructional steps consist of educational alternatives adaptive to the performance profile of each student.* These alternatives should include provisions for independent study, group study, laboratory experience, etc. The range of educational opportunities, including instructional materials and procedures, that need to be made available in a particular school is a matter to be determined by experience and study. In many ways, the materials are a key for providing an individualized program that is both workable and economically feasible. In the more conventional teacher-directed programs, it is possible to use textbooks and materials which permit the teacher to explain procedures and operations before the pupils begin their study. However, in individualized programs, the materials have to be developed in keeping with subject matter requirements geared to a variety of learning styles and providing for some degree of self-study. Unless this option is available, the amount of teacher help needed would be unmanageable even with the pupil-teacher ratio of 20 to 1. This does not mean, even when materials for self-study or independent study are available, that such materials and techniques should be exclusively employed. It does mean, however, that without the availability of self-study materials, group instruction or tutoring are the only techniques possible. For this reason, the LRDC emphasis related to materials design has been on the development of materials that can be self-instructional.

Materials Development

The approach to materials development at the LRDC is an ever-changing process, with the procedures used undergoing constant revision and refinement. The state of the art of developing materials necessary for individualized instruction is still in its infant stages. At best, what it represents is an attempt to provide materials that can reflect the general options that can help students to achieve the common goals. Therefore, the following description of present procedures for materials development[3] represents only our *current* thinking in this area and must be further refined and delineated by research and development.

Specifying and sequencing the instructional objectives of a unit.

Step 1. The initial step in materials development requires the writer to carefully review the curriculum outline which specifies the objectives included in each unit of the curriculum. In most cases this review includes further work in clarifying the exact nature of the ability represented by each of the objectives. A facilitating activity is the specification, where possible, of the test items to be used on the pre- and posttests for each objective within the curriculum. As the writer moves from the overall perspective of the curriculum to the preparation of materials for a particular "unit," he must analyze the unit to determine if the necessary prerequisites have received adequate attention in the earlier portions of the curriculum. This task takes on the characteristics of "task analysis," resulting in a possible ordering of the objectives within the unit.

Step 2. The second step in the developmental process requires a lesson rationale for each of the objectives in the unit. The content of the lesson rationale[4] usually includes the following: (1) a statement of the terminal behavior to be achieved (this statement is taken from the list of objectives comprising the curriculum); (2) an example of the terminal behavior to be displayed by the student; (3) a listing and explanation of the immediate instructional objectives; (4) a listing of the sequence of detailed steps (stated as observable pupil behaviors) through which lessons will take the student in going from the prerequisite abilities to the terminal behaviors; (5) a short description of type of lesson (paper-pencil response, a reading plus a worksheet, an experiment or laboratory experience plus a response sheet, taped or recorded lessons, films, filmstrips plus response sheets, etc.); (6) the logic or process of instruction (exercises involving small steps, general discussion or explanation plus follow-up exercises, inductive presentation or deductive presentation, etc.). The purpose of this rationale is to guide the writer in thinking specifically about how he plans to structure his lessons. Since most of the materials development and lesson development for the individualized program at the LRDC involves a team of developers, the rationale serves as a basis for in-house discussion. The rationale for a lesson developed for a particular unit (e.g., a unit in mathematics) is first of all reviewed by the particular curriculum staff, refined and expanded, and then shared with other staff members from other curriculum areas as well as other members of the LRDC staff for criticism and comments.

Step 3. After the lesson rationale has been sufficiently reviewed, the next step is to develop the first prototype lesson as specified in the rationale. When a team is involved in the development of lessons—materials that are to fit together into a total program—it is essential that all members of this team follow certain standard procedures regarding format, style and language. Without this, students and teachers encounter unnecessary difficulties in moving from lesson to lesson and unit to unit. A second reason for the consistency of format for each of the types and kinds of lessons is the concern for more widespread use of the lesson once it has been initially tested. For instance, taped lessons should adhere to the characteristics of the hardware presently available. Suggested additions of hardware must be carefully reviewed by all members of the curriculum staffs before incorporating them into the program. After the prototype lesson has been developed and before it is tried out with students, it is again reviewed by other members of the curriculum team.

Step 4—Pre-tryout. This involves the testing of the lesson with one or two children who may or may not have experienced similar types of lessons before. This is actually a laboratory test and is usually done before investing a lot of time and effort in tapes, art work and printing of multiple copies.

Step 5—Revision. Each pre-tryout stage is followed by an initial revision of the lesson.

Step 6—Field Trial. Actual field trial is not undertaken until the writer knows that his lesson will work with one or two students. Field tryouts involve a small group of students working independently but in an observed situation that can provide more extensive feedback relative to each student's success or lack of success with the lesson.

Step 7—Revision and In-context Tryout. Following the feedback from the field tryout, the lesson is then revised and put together with a larger sequence of lessons for classroom tryout. The in-context tryout is still considered developmental, thus providing the need for formative evaluation of the more complete package. A major purpose of this stage is to examine the effectiveness of the materials in the context of an individualized instruction setting.

An example of the type of lesson used in the LRDC individualized instruction program may be helpful in clarifying the materials development steps just discussed. The sample lesson is from a unit on beginning fractions. As with all lessons, an attempt was made to provide materials that require as little teacher involvement as possible so that the teacher can work with individual students and with small groups while all students are actively involved in learning. Figure 1 is a portion of the unit flow chart used in the mathematics program. This chart suggests to the teacher that once the student has completed Units 1 through 7, the student should have the prerequisites necessary to begin work in Unit 11, Beginning Fractions. Figure 2 shows the sequencing arrangement of the nine objectives that comprise this particular unit. The purpose of the unit is to introduce the student to fractional parts of a whole. This whole can be either a region or a set of objects. As in previous units, equivalence is a major concept and relates most directly to the units of Beginning Addition and Subtraction.

Materials available are the following: (1) tests, both pre- and posttests, (2) a lesson booklet, (3) a "lesson box," and (4) a wide variety of mathematics tools and devices not specific to a given lesson but general to all. A pretest of all objectives in the unit is administered before starting the unit. The test can be given either orally or in written form. It is used as a basis for deciding where the student will begin. After the student has completed those lessons in the unit deemed necessary for him, he then completes a posttest.

The "lesson booklet"[5] for this unit is a 21-page booklet designed to be used as an option for those students who (1) have

1971-1972 Individualized Math Continuum Flow Chart

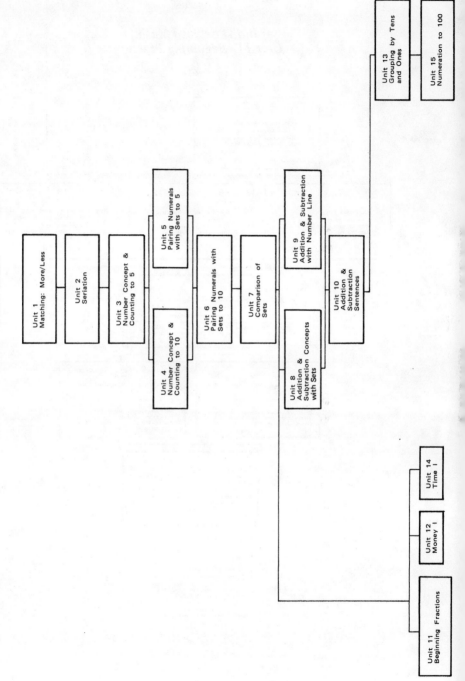

Figure 2

Individualized Math:
Unit 11–Beginning Fractions

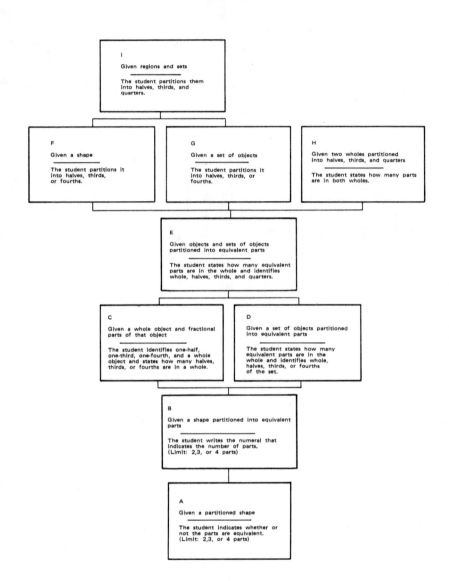

I

Given regions and sets

The student partitions them into halves, thirds, and quarters.

F

Given a shape

The student partitions it into halves, thirds, or fourths.

G

Given a set of objects

The student partitions it into halves, thirds, or fourths.

H

Given two wholes partitioned into halves, thirds, and quarters

The student states how many parts are in both wholes.

E

Given objects and sets of objects partitioned into equivalent parts

The student states how many equivalent parts are in the whole and identifies whole, halves, thirds, and quarters.

C

Given a whole object and fractional parts of that object

The student identifies one-half, one-third, one-fourth, and a whole object and states how many halves, thirds, or fourths are in a whole.

D

Given a set of objects partitioned into equivalent parts

The student states how many equivalent parts are in the whole and identifies whole, halves, thirds, or fourths of the set.

B

Given a shape partitioned into equivalent parts

The student writes the numeral that indicates the number of parts. (Limit: 2,3, or 4 parts)

A

Given a partitioned shape

The student indicates whether or not the parts are equivalent. (Limit: 2,3, or 4 parts)

some degree of reading proficiency, (2) can follow a few simple directions, (3) can attend to a task for an extended period of time, and (4) can write responses when requested. The first three or four pages of the booklet include introductory exercises and a review of prerequisite concepts. The next set of pages might be termed the "instructional pages" and is designed to lead the student by means of a series of small tasks to mastery of the general concept of equivalent parts. The remaining pages in the booklet might be termed "practice." They can be used for both practice and review, depending on the needs of the student. The booklet also contains two curriculum-embedded tests which are check tests to assist the student and teacher in determining when the child has reached the desired proficiency.

The "lesson box" is a small box of materials consisting of (1) ten cards made of heavy cardboard, each with a geometric figure, some divided into equivalent parts and some not, (2) a bag containing a variety of colored shapes that can be used to match the shapes on the ten cards, and (3) directions to the teacher concerning how the student is to match the colored shapes to the geometric figures. Suggested questions that the teacher would ask the student upon completion of this manipulative task include the following:

    (1)   How do you know that these are the same size parts?

    (2)   How many pieces are in this whole?

    (3)   Are all the parts of this whole the same size?

This alternative set of materials requires less reading and writing than other parts of the unit. Each task within this lesson is designed to be completed in a relatively short period of time, either by a student working independently or by a group of students working with the teacher.

Additional options for individual students are formed by combining portions of the lesson box and the lesson booklet—for example, for students who are just beginning to write. Such students might begin with the lesson box and then work on selected portions of the booklet, with the booklet being used in this case as a teaching aid to assist the student in learning to follow written directions and in responding in a paper-pencil fashion.

Because this lesson was developed for children between the ages of five and eight, the lesson options are decided jointly by the teacher and the child, with the major weight of decision-making on the shoulders of the teacher.

Summary

In order for individual students to be able to realize the overall goals of education, these goals must be further defined in terms of objectives that are common to all students and objectives that can vary from student to student. Materials, resources and the instructional environment are all important aspects of the means of achieving these goals. Until recently, the means to achieve these educational goals have been so limited as to create an educational system that is more involved in screening than in educating students. One important aspect of individualized instruction programs is the provision for establishing means that are not overly dependent on time and management procedures for student accomplishments. However, to remove these constraints means that materials and resources must be developed (1) that can provide for a variety of individual differences, (2) that can be utilized in a variety of instructional settings, and (3) that are appropriate for individual as well as group learning activities. It is toward these goals of materials development that the Learning Research and Development Center at the University of Pittsburgh has been working for the past nine years.

Notes

1. Quoted by David Elkind. Johnny and the Nursery School—Jean Piaget. *New York Times Magazine,* May 26, 1968, p. 80.
2. J.O. Bolvin and R. Glaser. Developmental Aspects of Individually Prescribed Instruction. *Audiovisual Instruction,* 1968, *13,* pp. 828-83.
3. C.M. Lindvall. *Lesson Writer's Manual,* Learning Research and Development Center, University of Pittsburgh, December 1969.
4. Adapted from LRDC form "Lesson Rationale," 1970.
5. The lesson booklets presently in use in the IPI mathematics program are booklets that have been developed jointly by the Learning Research and Development Center of the University of Pittsburgh and Research of Better Schools, Philadelphia.

John O. Bolvin is Associate Director, Learning Research and Development Center, University of Pittsburgh, Pennsylvania.

An Instructional Module Design

Richard W. Burns

Educators are constantly seeking to improve both the *means* and the *ends* of education. At times the two appear to be closely related (as when thinking about methods and content) and, conversely, at other times means and ends are quite clearly separated. It is often difficult to decide whether the educator ought to concentrate on improving the ends, or whether the ends adequately represent societal expectations and the educator ought to focus on improving education by improving the means.

Efforts to improve the means of instruction have not borne great fruit and today many teachers are employing means hardly distinguishable from those employed in the 1800s. Additionally, efforts to demonstrate (prove) that pictures are better than verbal symbols, rereading is better than reading once, underlining will improve remembering, note taking is a valid method to improve recall, outlining enhances retention, drill materials X are better than Y, and other similar studies of teaching and learning strategies have generally resulted in failure. That is, no one method of teaching nor any one method of learning has been identified as having clear superiority over any other method for all students. One is generally led to the conclusion that searching for such a panacea is a waste of time and effort.

It can be observed, however, that the things that "work," that is, the methods and strategies which have some proven value in enabling learners to learn, do have elements in common. These include individual pacing, feedback and reinforcement. We find such elements in tutoring, programmed instruction and computer assisted instruction. Additionally, there is an abundance of hard evidence to show that people vary in their learning ability, mode of learning, study habits, interests, amount learned about given topics, skill development, motor ability, productivity on jobs, language development, etc. Considering all the elements of physical health, mental health, personality, mental capacity, motor ability, etc., the uniqueness of humans is an inescapable fact. If we then turn to the basic biologic nature of man and attend carefully to the authoritative evidence, we just might become convinced of and espouse the principle that "no two living things are alike."

Now, if we add all of this together, what do we get? We seem to discover and rediscover the fact that learning is an individual process. This leads directly to individualized instruction (I-I) as perhaps the one and only *means* to whatever *ends* society decides are worthy, achievable goals (objectives) of education. However, I-I as a general description of how humans go about learning is not specific enough from the teacher's point of view to enable him or her to implement learning in the classroom.

If one were to stop at this point (consideration of the evidence) and try to diagram how learning takes place and then further diagram how this would occur for 30 unique students all at the same time, he would conclude:

A.   Thirty bodies would require 30 methods.
B.   There is no way a group diagram could be drawn to account for all contingencies.

I suspect that carried to the extreme, I-I means as many methods as learners. However, in practice we might suspect that some differences concerning learning interests and styles are small, so that some prescribed strategies would be effective for the majority of learners.

To implement I-I, many instructional schemes (devices, strategies, packages) could be and have been developed to aid the learner in effective (efficient in terms of time, cost, effort and result) learning. Whatever these schemes are, they will, in order to be effective, have to do the following:

1.   Consider the learner's interest

2. Consider the learner's readiness
3. Consider the learner's rate of learning (time)
4. Consider the learner's repertoire of habits (scope and sequence) that he applies to learning (study habits)
5. Provide the learner with success
6. Provide the learner with corrective feedback (or knowledge of the results of his learning)
7. Provide the learner with knowledge of cognitive and psychomotor goals (there may be reservations relative to this notion with regard to some affective goals, and this point is further elaborated upon later in this paper).

Instructional modules (IMs) are one type of package (scheme) for implementing I-I which incorporates the features outlined above. *An IM is a structured sequence of learning events designed to accommodate the attainment, on the part of the learner, of a wide range of objectives.* Of course, any specific IM is designed to accomplish a limited number of terminal behavioral objectives as stated in the module. Even IMs vary in their formats, and the remainder of this article describes one type of IM with which the Curriculum and Instruction Department of The University of Texas at El Paso has had extensive, successful experience.

The format of the UTEP-IM generally has these parts:

1. Title page
2. Objectives
3. Overview
4. Pretest
5. Rationale
6. Instructional Alternatives
7. Posttest
8. Resources

Title Page

This page gives source credit, date, title and IM code number.

Objectives

This section contains written terminal behavior objectives (TBOs) in a style readily comprehended by the learner. They are concise statements of what the learner is expected to *do* at the end of the module. Instructional objectives (IOs), or "enabling objectives," as they are termed by some educators, are not listed, although the module creator would have developed and used IOs in creating the IM. Some IMs which in whole or in part are designed to effect learning of affective objectives (attitudes, appreciations and interests) are modified so that they *do not* list selected TBOs. The reasoning behind this modification is that the inclusion of some objectives may impede or even prevent their attainment. For example, if the attitude "religious tolerance" is the substance of the objective, and if any learner really felt protective (for whatever reason) of his present intolerant attitude, the purpose of the IM would be defeated by including the objective.

It has been argued that the exclusion of the learner from knowledge of affective objectives violates the commonly accepted notions that (1) objectives should be made public, (2) objectives should be known to the learner, and (3) learners knowing objectives will attain them more effectively. These notions generally hold for cognitive and psychomotor objectives. Then the argument continues with—well, if this is true for the cognitive and psychomotor areas, why not for the affective? Many affective objectives can be made known and the learning will proceed more effectively when this is done. There is a difference between the cognitive, psychomotor and affective areas, and this difference accounts for the fact that often feelings can be altered or acquired (emotions learned) more readily when the goal is unknown to the learner. It is inherent in the nature of the affective domain.

Overview

Some IMs contain an overview section, while others skip it, depending on the nature of the module. Whether or not the overview is present usually depends on the nature of the pretest. One function of the overview is to increase the likelihood that the learner will meet the criteria inherent in the pretest if he knows (understands) the content. Most learners do not successfully meet the criteria of pretests. In fact, in a modularized learning program, the learners often "give up trying" on the pretests and go from *objectives* directly to *rationale,* since experience tells them that the "pretests are impossible" so "why bother." One reason for this extremely low rate of success with "testing out" of IMs resides with the unique and varied vocabulary, testing and writing styles of the module creators. The problem frequently results from the fact that the individual learner acquired his behavior in a different school, or under the direction of a different person, or from reading a different source, written at a time when a different terminology was in vogue. Any of these factors alone or in combination may cause the learner to be "thrown off" enough so that he can't pass the pretest, even though he understands the basic concepts which the pretest is designed to measure. In such cases, the overview is designed to refresh the learner, clarify vocabulary terms, and establish a set for the learner who basically knows the material. For the learner who is unfamiliar with the content, the overview then serves as a preview of that content.

Pretest

Pretests can serve several purposes, but in the sense used here the basic purpose is to determine whether or not the learner needs the coming instruction. If the learner already has, as part of his behavior repertoire, the behaviors to be developed by the IM, then he should be allowed to "skip" the module and proceed to the next one. The pretest is a criterion test designed to determine if the learner has met or exceeded the performances as specified by the terminal behavioral objectives of the IM.

Pretests can also be designed as readiness tests to determine if the learner possesses the necessary prerequisite behaviors that will be demanded by the IM. In a training or educational program which contains a series of modules, this function is of decreasing significance, especially if there is a required or suggested sequence of IMs. With sequencing, prior IMs obviously would be developing the behaviors needed in subsequent modules, and criterion testing assures that the learner does in fact possess the prerequisite behaviors.

Rationale

If the learner reaches the rationale section, he needs the IM in the sense that he does not possess the behaviors to be developed by the module. However, the learner may not perceive that *he* needs the module. That is, he may have little or no desire to acquire the behaviors. The function of the rationale is to state the fundamental reasons for the module, its importance, and *why* the learner should achieve the objectives as stated.

Instructional Alternatives

Instructional alternatives are the heart of the IM. Since the major purpose of the IM is to assist in individualizing instruction, several alternative learning strategies should be provided. The visual reading, visual non-reading, and auditory modes are the most frequently provided instructional options structured for the learner, from which he is expected to select one. Readings, film strips, slide-tapes, tapes and lecture-seminars are the media most frequently selected, alone or in combination, to provide the instructional options. Two reading options are often provided in one IM, one textual and one authored by the creator of the module. The latter is frequently the most economical from the learner's point of view, since the material is written specifically for the module and it need contain no extraneous content. Another option often included is a "do your own thing" variety, which places the burden of learning on the learner, who can then prepare for the posttest in any way his heart desires. Options may or may not include live instructors, guest speakers, discussion groups, etc., but the majority of the options are purposefully designed to exploit independent study. In any case, there is always a *module director* available for counseling and consultation. It is well to remember that the IM, and especially the instructional alternatives, are designed to provide for a variety of learning abilities, modes, study habits, interests, language levels and information backgrounds. Actually there is no limit to the number and variety of alternatives that can be provided—it is up to the module author to determine the number and types of strategies offered for learning.

Posttest

The posttest is a criterion measure designed to require the learner to perform or demonstrate the behaviors as specifically stated in the objectives. Like the pretest, the learner meets or exceeds or does not meet (let's avoid the term "fail") the criteria. If he meets the criteria, he has finished the module and is credited with the appropriate behaviors. If he does not meet the criteria, he may repeat the same instructional alternative in its entirety, may repeat it in part, select another alternative, or consult with the module director to select some other effective course of action. He may repeat the same or an alternative equivalent posttest as many times as is consistent with the system philosophy.

Resources

The section on resources is designed to list and enable the learner to locate all the materials and media devices required to successfully complete the module. The list may include such things as books, other textual materials, slides, tapes, films, maps, charts, diagrams, projectors, recorders, etc.

This section may also contain a list of suggested further readings if desired. These readings should be selected to assist in clarifying the objectives or to promote their acquisition rather than being a comprehensive bibliography of the subject of the module.

Additional IM Characteristics

The pre- and posttest, being criterion tests and having a 1:1 relationship with the objectives (each objective is measured by some test), may at times be exactly alike. This is usually true when the objective involves a psychomotor skill, but it is also not uncommon with cognitive learnings. When the test items are verbal items (multiple choice, essay, completion, alternative choice, short answer, matching, etc.) there is a greater opportunity to develop different but equivalent pre- and posttests. When the test items are processes and products, the pre- and posttests are likely to be the same.

IMs may be of any length, usually requiring from about

one-half hour to 15 hours to complete. Some modules, when coupled with extended field experience activity, may require a number of weeks to complete. Also, some IMs may be highly structured while others are only loosely structured. For example, if for some reason it would be desirable for each learner to be required to experience selected, specific activities, the module may provide only limited options in the instructional alternatives section. This type of highly structured module tends to violate the concept of I-I and should be used sparingly. At the other extreme are modules so loose that they permit the learner wide latitude, even to the extent of devising his own goals and selecting his own experiences to accomplish them.

Our experience at UTEP with IMs has shown them to be highly adaptable to a wide range of subject matter, numerous learning strategies and, most importantly, to learner needs.

Richard W. Burns is Professor of Education at the University of Texas at El Paso.

Personalized Instruction
or
What to do when they put a number on the back of your sport coat, issue you a bullhorn and schedule your class in the football stadium

David G. Born and Steven Zlutnick

Educators are in general agreement that to be optimally effective, educational programs should be tailored to individual students. This is not to say that the objectives and content of each course of study should be different for each student, but rather that the educational program should capitalize on the (usually) highly individual interests of students. Further, it must be recognized that there is an astonishing range of academic skills among students in the typical university classroom. An ideal educational program makes use of strengths and promotes development in areas of academic weakness.

Although the need for individualizing educational programs has been recognized at the level of primary and secondary grades, that need also exists at the level of college instruction, where individual differences are exaggerated as students prepare for careers requiring widely divergent skills. Unfortunately, the "monster" class of 500 students has grown increasingly common on college campus across the country and will likely become more common, as educators struggle to handle larger classes at a time when state legislators increasingly tighten the purse-strings on university budgets.

A major deterrent to individualizing college instruction is the high ratio of students to faculty teaching hours. That ratio might be altered either by drastically reducing student admissions or by markedly increasing the number of existing faculty members. Unfortunately, neither of these alternatives would appear to be desirable or reasonable under existing social and economic circumstances. Fortunately, an alternative has recently emerged.

Fred S. Keller (1966, 1968), professor emeritus at Columbia University, has described a personalized system of instruction (PSI) in which undergraduate students perform in "instructional" roles. Although more will be said about these instructional roles in a later section of this article, the reader will note that to the extent that students may be used to assume instructional assignments it should be possible to greatly alter the student/ "teacher" ratio without the hiring of additional university faculty. By lowering this ratio, education may be made more personal and differences among students may be minimized as academic deficiencies are diagnosed and remedial programs are designed. In essence PSI strives to make students more alike—by making them all excellent.

Keller's system differs in a number of ways from the traditional college lecture course. First, there is a sharp de-emphasis on the lecture as a vehicle for presenting new information and/or ideas to students. In PSI all materials that are sufficiently important for a student to study are made available to him in a carefully written form. Although lectures are occasionally delivered, students are typically not held responsible for lecture content—because the purpose of lectures is mainly to supplement and provide further illustration of points made in the written material. A second way in which PSI differs from more traditional instruction is that the bulk of class time is spent in administering examinations over small portions of course material and providing immediate feedback to students about their mastery of that material. Third, there is often a requirement that examinations are successfully completed only when a student writes a perfect paper. Failure to demonstrate complete mastery means simply that the student re-studies the same material and reports to class at a later time to take a different examination over the same material. Students who have not thoroughly mastered a unit of course material are not penalized by having their grade lowered. Rather, their progress through the course material is held up until they successfully remediate and demonstrate mastery on a second or third examination. A fourth way in which PSI differs from more traditional courses is that students may move through course material largely at their own rate. By having approximately twice as many days set aside for students to take examinations as there are examinations to be taken and by tying course completion to thorough mastery of written content, it is possible for students to fill course requirements in less than the usual academic term. Finally, in a PSI course, written examination performance is evaluated in the presence of the student during the same hour in which the examination was taken, and the evaluation includes an interview with the student over the course material comprising the unit.

Classroom Mechanics

The procedures used in a PSI course are perhaps best illustrated by describing the operation of a specific course.* The general objectives of Psychology 101, the beginning psychology course at the University of Utah, are to train students to speak and write the language of modern psychology and to develop sufficient understanding of psychological principles that students can prescribe procedures for developing and controlling some simple human behaviors. Such beginning courses, most often having an enrollment of approximately 150 students, typically meet Monday through Friday, one hour per day, for the regular ten or eleven week academic quarter. On the first day of class each student receives a detailed statement of course policies and procedures and a course calendar which identifies the activities scheduled in the classroom for each day of the academic quarter (i.e., the topic and date of each lecture, film, or demonstration, and the days set aside for test taking). To make certain that students thoroughly understand course procedures, they are asked to take a short quiz over the course policies and procedures statement on the following class day.

*A more detailed statement of the philosophy and operation of a PSI course, including sample materials, is available in two training manuals which may be purchased from the College Bookstore, 200 University, Salt Lake City, Utah 84112: *Instructor Manual for Development of a Personalized Instruction Course* (165 pp.), $6.25, and *Proctor Manual* (44 pp.), $2.25.

On the second day of class each student is assigned a proctor who will evaluate his examinations throughout the remainder of the course. The proctor is most often a junior or senior psychology major. Each proctor is assigned eight to ten students. After the proctor assignments have been made, each student reports to his proctor. The proctor answers any questions about course operation and then administers the quiz over course policies and procedures (mentioned above) to students who indicate they are ready to take that examination. In addition to providing an opportunity for students to evaluate their understanding of how the course operates, this first quiz acquaints the student with the proctor and with the testing procedure which will be used in later evaluations of his course mastery. As each student completes the examination, he brings it to the proctor, who quickly examines the written answers, asks for clarification if appropriate and evaluates the student's understanding of the course procedures. Students who successfully pass the policies and procedures quiz are then congratulated by the proctors and given a study guide for use in preparing for the first unit mastery test.

Course Materials

The written course material is packaged in twelve units plus two unit review tests and a comprehensive final examination. A typical unit consists of an assigned number of written pages for study, a unit study guide and several alternate forms of examinations over that course material.

Study Guides. Each unit study guide specifies the reading assignment for the student and is followed by a short introduction to the subject matter comprising the unit. This introduction may include information which is supplemental to material being used in textbooks and/or it may be designed to bridge units and relate them to one another. Following the unit introduction is a lengthy list of study items. The purpose of the study items is twofold. First, by designing a study item for each portion of the written material sufficiently important for the student to master, one can prevent the student from overlooking essential material. Second, properly constructed study guide items will lead the student to the appropriate kind of preparation for the subject matter involved. For example, "Be prepared to describe the operation of a carburetor" will probably call for a different type of preparation than the item, "Be able to identify the parts of a carburetor," or "Given the tools and components, be prepared to assemble a carburetor." In essence, the study items are the behavioral objectives of the course.

Unit Tests. A unit test is designed to take approximately ten to fifteen minutes to complete. Each test question requires a written answer from the student and the answers themselves may range from a single term to a short paragraph. The individual items on the tests are made up from the list of unit study guide items, thereby guaranteeing consistency between how the student has been asked to prepare and how he is in fact examined.

Testing Procedures

When a student feels that he has thoroughly mastered the course material in a unit, he reports to class on a testing day and requests the proper unit examination from the person in charge of course materials. Upon receiving that examination he takes a seat in a section of the classroom set aside for students completing examinations. After answering each question he reports to a different area of the classroom reserved for evaluation and discussion of examinations. There he is greeted by his proctor and the evaluation begins.

Proctors are required to provide the student with feedback about each examination item and to mark each written answer as correct, incorrect or ambiguous. If an answer is wrong the student is informed of his error and may then be asked to tell the proctor what he knows about the subject matter of the question. (The reader should note that the test questions are not identical to the study guide items.) Such quizzing may reveal a misunderstanding of the question or a misunderstanding in the student's preparation for the mastery test. If this quizzing reveals insufficient or inappropriate mastery of course material, the student may be directed to complete a specific remedial task that is to be brought in and checked by the proctor before the student takes a second unit mastery test over the material. If on the other hand the error resulted from a misreading of the test question or a misunderstanding of the test question, the student may be asked to sit down and write an appropriate answer to the question.

Even if the student shows written mastery of the course material called for by the examination items, the proctor is instructed to engage the students in conversation in connection with one or more of those test items. Sometimes this may be accomplished by asking the student to give an example of an item or principle which he has correctly identified or described, or he may be asked to provide further detail about an example which he has given in answer to an item. The purpose of this interview is to develop verbal skills to the point where students may speak as well as write the language of psychology. Further, by providing some impromptu questions the proctor and the student have an opportunity to form a more thorough evaluation of the student's mastery of course material. Such questions also discourage collusion among students about specific test items and encourage broader preparation for the mastery tests than might otherwise occur.

If the student successfully passes the unit mastery test, he is congratulated by the proctor, given the next unit study guide, and encouraged to complete the new unit's work at an early date. If, on the other hand, the student's performance on the mastery test was not adequate, the proctor has the responsibility for recommending remedial steps to the student which, if completed, will assure his mastery of the material at the necessary level. Should the student fail to pass his second unit mastery test, a proctor may try to schedule an individual tutoring session with the student. During this session they will carefully go over the answers the student has prepared to the study questions in an effort to establish the very thorough comprehension required to pass a unit mastery test. If this does not result in the necessary level of competence, the case is referred to the instructor for special consultation.

Role of the Instructional Staff
Course Instruction. An instructor who adopts PSI will find

that he has a number of duties to fulfill which are not required in a more traditional lecture course. One of his first tasks involves the reading, evaluation and selection of textbooks and related course materials. Since it is unlikely that any textbook will meet all of an instructor's educational needs, PSI requires that he eliminate or rewrite any portions of the text that he feels to be inadequate or incomplete.

Once he is satisfied with the quality of the reading materials, the PSI instructor faces the most time-consuming job of all— preparing the unit study guides and unit examinations. The preparedness of the student depends in large part on the quality of the study guide. The study guide is the instrument through which the instructor communicates to the student what he needs to master and how he should be prepared to demonstrate mastery. If the guide is vague or ambiguous, the student will find himself faced with the familiar problem of trying to second-guess the instructor.

Unit exams must correspond to the unit study guides, and the instructor must prepare at least two reliable alternate forms (i.e., three exams per unit) to allow the student the necessary opportunities to repeat examinations in the event of poor performance. Thus, if a typical course consists of approximately 15 units, the instructor must prepare 15 unit study guides, 45 unit exams and a comprehensive final exam.

Because lectures are eliminated as a *primary* source of course content, the instructor must carefully plan the nature of the supplementary course activities, usually occurring twice weekly. It is here that he may compress his very best lecture material into a few intermittently scheduled lectures. In addition, he must select and schedule films and guest speakers and arrange for any special demonstrations. Once the instructor has evaluated the text, determined the number of study units and test days and established a schedule of lectures, guest speakers, films and demonstrations, he must summarize this information in a course calendar which is distributed to students at the beginning of the term.

Also in advance of the course, the instructor must choose a

course assistant and proctors. This often proves to be difficult because he must find students who have time for the very thorough preparation required. They must also be very familiar with the course content and have the ability to work well with other students. In advance of the first class meeting he must initiate a training program which will guarantee that his proctor staff is thoroughly acquainted with both their duties and their responsibilities to students. In addition, with regular proctor meetings during the academic term the instructor will attempt to guarantee that each proctor has the level of subject matter expertise required by his position in the course.

By relieving the instructor of the job of delivering daily lectures of dubious value or interest, PSI permits him to discover and tend to the individual needs of his students. During testing sessions (three days per week) he is available in the classroom to those students who wish to interact with him on an informal basis. During these sessions he may also seek out students who are doing either exceptionally well in the course or who need special help. It is this new accessibility of the instructor and his increased opportunity for interaction with students that help to make the course more personal and rewarding for all concerned.

Course Assistant. The course assistant acts in two capacities: (1) He serves as a teaching apprentice to the course instructor, and (2) he helps to relieve the instructor of some of the pressure of the large number of social contacts in a course with, say, 15 proctors and 150 students. The course assistant's duties may include dealing with various student problems (or he at least mediates them for the instructor), directing the materials supervisor, supervising the proctors and providing special tutorial help for students having difficulties. He may also assist the proctors in the event that a test session is particularly overloaded with students.

Proctors. The proctors comprise the heart of a PSI course because they are directly responsible for the daily progress of the student. In many respects it is the proctor staff which determines the success or failure of a PSI course. In addition to being a "teacher," the proctor often finds himself in the role of tutor, friend, confidant and mother hen. And, it should be noted, the course instructor and assistant encourage such relationships. Many students are surprised to receive a phone call from their proctor inquiring about their inattendance at the past few testing sessions. The proctor has a responsibility to keep abreast of the progress of all of his students to prevent them from falling too far behind, to provide special tutorial assistance to them if needed and to go to any lengths necessary (short of blackmail) to keep them coming to class and fulfilling the course requirements. At the same time he must maintain the high standards of excellence required by the instructor.

Selection and Training of Staff

Course Assistant. The course assistant is generally a graduate teaching assistant, or a graduate student interested in PSI. He should be thoroughly familiar with the course content and he should be able to interact easily with other people because he will have a great deal of contact with students and the proctor staff. The selection of a course assistant who has previously served as a proctor has many obvious advantages; he will be in a much better position to understand and anticipate difficulties encountered by the proctors.

The course assistant should have a relationship with the instructor resembling an apprentice-colleague. Within such a relationship the assistant will develop a repertoire of behaviors on both technical and practical levels. By observing the instructor in day-to-day interactions with students and administrators, he will learn many of the skills necessary to deal with problems arising within the PSI format. In addition, through constant analysis and discussion of strategies with the instructor, he will acquire the technical know-how to develop and maintain his own PSI course.

Proctors. Proctors may be selected from a number of different populations. One of the best sources, particularly if a general or survey course is involved, is graduate students who need to review for comprehensive examinations. Another source is graduate students interested in teaching PSI courses when they become faculty members. However, the greatest pool of potential proctors is made up of the superior undergraduates who have previously completed the same PSI course. To the extent that these people have been thoroughly trained as students taking the course they should be capable of assuming the proctor role with a minimum of difficulty.

Proctors can be trained in a variety of ways. As former students, they are already familiar with the general style and mannerisms of their own proctor. Specific strategies and procedures can be examined and discussed during a one- or two-day workshop prior to the beginning of the term and frequent meetings (at least once per week) while the course is in progress. Also, much important training can be provided with on-the-job monitoring of proctor-student interactions by the course instructor and assistant. Because they are frequently located in and around the evaluation area, the instructor and assistant can eavesdrop unobtrusively during proctor-student interactions and can provide prompt feedback to the proctor at the completion of the session.

All potential proctors, regardless of their class standing, grade point average, previous experience and final grade in the course, should be required to take the unit and final exams to demonstrate proficiency with the course material before they are allowed to evaluate student examinations. Proctors who have not mastered a key principle or concept will not be able to help a student having difficulty with the same concept. However, because the course instructor and assistant are readily available in the classroom, a proctor can always call upon them for help if the need arises.

We have found in the past that it is not necessary to pay proctors for their services. The practice adopted by the present authors and others (e.g., Keller, 1968; Malott and Svinicki, 1969), has been to allow the proctor to sign up for a Special Projects course. The credit the proctor receives is approximately equal to the credit hours of the course itself, and is justified by the intense preparation and active learning engaged in by each proctor. In addition to course credit, the proctor is able to establish a close personal relationship with the instructor and other good students, he gets recognition for his outstanding past performance as a student, and he has an opportunity to do something meaningful for fellow students.

Evaluation of Course Objectives

Because relaxed and informal relationships typically develop between a proctor and his students, the proctor is in an excellent position to determine the quality of academic behaviors produced under PSI. The proctors, then, provide the first and most effective means of determining whether course objectives are being met. A second determination of the program's success in achieving course objectives is made by the course instructor. Although it is not possible for the instructor and course assistant to monitor each proctor-student interaction, the individual unit mastery tests are retained, and they can be spot-checked to evaluate the proctor scoring of written student responses. Should a proctor decision about a written answer come in question, the matter is discussed with the proctor to determine if the proctor has erred in his evaluation. This inspection of written exams provides both an opportunity to determine if high quality written answers are being produced and a further quality control check on the proctor staff. Less formal information about the program's effectiveness is obtained by the instructor as he roams the classroom on testing days discussing course procedures and course content with students. The instructor's final check on the effectiveness of his PSI program is the comprehensive written final examination, which is not repeatable and which he alone administers and evaluates.

Comparisons of PSI with the More
Traditional College Lecture Course

Although few formal comparisons of PSI and lecture-type instruction have been made, several investigations (e.g., Born, Gledhill and Davis, 1972; McMichael and Corey, 1969; Sheppard and MacDermot, 1970) have reported superior terminal examination performance by students completing PSI courses. Corey, McMichael and Tremont (1969) have also reported superior retention of material mastered in the context of a PSI course. Furthermore, a number of investigators (e.g., Born and Herbert, 1971; Gallup, 1970) have reported that students evaluate the PSI procedures very favorably even though courses taught in this manner demand a great deal of work.

In addition to superior levels of student performance, correspondingly higher grades and favorable course ratings, PSI courses may also be characterized by a substantially greater number of student withdrawals than occur in comparable lecture courses (Born, 1971). Although PSI procedures would seem ideal for students who have a history of difficulty with academic subjects (i.e., low cumulative grade point averages), it is precisely this group of students who withdraw from PSI courses (Born, 1971). However, the reader should note that these students do not seem to withdraw because they have special difficulty meeting the high mastery criteria associated with unit examinations. Rather, when working at their own rate, they do not pace themselves properly, fall steadily behind as the academic term progresses and finally withdraw.

Concluding Remarks

A number of published reports have recently become available indicating successful application of PSI procedures to a wide range of subject matter areas. In addition to courses in psychology, there have been applications in physics (Green, n.d.), astronomy (Dessler, 1971), engineering (Hoberock, 1971; Koen, 1970), mathematics (Newman, McKean and Purtle, 1971) and many others. Furthermore, commercially prepared materials are now available for a variety of courses, including anthropology, Spanish, English composition, informal logic, biology and sociology.* Finally, Greenspoon (1971) has recently reported that approximately half of the course offerings at Temple Buell College are now cast in a general PSI format.

Based on preliminary reports, PSI procedures appear to be a resounding success, and students trained under the system are among its most outspoken advocates. However, the system described in this article will not find direct application to all educational settings. For example, it is not necessary to train and supervise a staff of proctors in classes with enrollments of 10-15

*Individual Learning Systems, Inc., San Rafael, California.

students; the instructor can probably function as a super-proctor and handle all of the instructional duties alone. At the other extreme, it is unlikely that the system described in this article will work well in a class with more than 150 students; the administrative duties imposed on the instructor begin to occupy much of the time he would otherwise spend in tending to and solving problems of his students. In short, PSI is not a panacea for very large classes, although an interesting offshoot of PSI, designed to handle 1000 students, has been reported by Malott and Svinicki (1969).

From the preceding comments it is apparent that PSI will probably not solve the problem of the instructor assigned a class in the football stadium or huge auditorium. For him there seem to be few alternatives. Although he can provide an array of lectures, films and demonstrations which are truly impressive to him and his colleagues, the fact that he is so greatly outnumbered during student contact hours makes it unlikely that he can gather much of the first-hand information he needs to evaluate the impact of his formal presentations on his students. In essence, he is forced to guess about his daily teaching effectiveness, and there is little he can do about that. Given the situation in which an instructor has a monster class, a large number of seemingly disinterested students and virtually no way to get the information he needs to improve the educational effectiveness of his course, he might turn his attention to a consideration of new ways to entertain his students when he assumes his assigned role on center stage. With luck his students might then leave the university with at least a few fond memories of their course in Colosseum 101. To this end we would recommend that the instructor find a good concessionaire, lots of pretty, scantily clad cheerleaders and a trained bear.

References

Born, D.G. Student Withdrawals in Personalized Instruction Courses and in Lecture Courses. In F. Newman (Chm.), Personalized Instruction: A National Trend Moves into the Rocky Mountain Region. Symposium presented at the meeting of the Rocky Mountain Psychological Association, Denver, May 1971.

Born, D.G., Gledhill, S.M. and Davis, M.L. Examination Performance in

Lecture-Discussion and Personalized Instruction Courses. *Journal of Applied Behavior Analysis,* 1972, in press.

Born, D.G. and Herbert, Emily W. A Further Study of Keller's Personalized System of Instruction. *Journal of Experimental Education,* 1971, *40,* 6-11.

Corey, J.R., McMichael, J.S. and Tremont, P.J. Long-Term Effects of Personalized Instruction in an Introductory Psychology Course. Paper presented at the meetings of the Midwestern Psychological Association, Chicago, Illinois, May 1969.

Dessler, A.J. Teaching Without Lectures. *Rice University Review,* 1971, *6,* 9-12.

Gallup, H.F. Individualized Instruction in an Introductory Psychology Course. Paper presented at the meeting of the Eastern Psychological Association, Atlantic City, New Jersey, April 1970.

Green, B.A. A Self-Paced Course in Freshman Physics. Occasional Paper No. 2 of the Education Research Center, Massachusetts Institute of Technology, Cambridge, Massachusetts, n.d.

Greenspoon, J. New Dimensions in Higher Education: The New College Program of Temple Buell College. In F. Newman (Chm.), Personalized Instruction: A National Trend Moves into the Rocky Mountain Region. Symposium presented at the meeting of the Rocky Mountain Psychological Association, Denver, May 1971.

Hoberock, L.L. Personalized Instruction in Mechanical Engineering. *Engineering Education,* March 1971.

Keller, Fred S. A Personal Course in Psychology. In R. Ulrich, T. Stachnik and J. Mabry (Eds.) *Control of Human Behavior.* Glenview, Illinois: Scott Foresman, Inc., 1966, 91-93.

Keller, Fred S. "Goodbye, Teacher . . ." *Journal of Applied Behavior Analysis,* 1968, *1,* 79-89.

Koen, B.V. Self-Paced Instruction for Engineering Students. *Engineering Education,* 1970, *60,* 735-736.

Malott, R.W. and Svinicki, J.G. Contingency Management in an Introductory Psychology Course for One Thousand Students. *Psychological Record,* 1969, *19,* 545-556.

McMichael, J.S. and Corey, J.R. Contingency Management in an Introductory Psychology Course Produces Better Learning. *Journal of Applied Behavior Analysis,* 1969, *2,* 79-83.

Newman, F.L., McKean, H. and Purtle, R. Personalized Instruction in a Three Semester Mathematics and Statistics Course. In F. Newman (Chm.), Personalized Instruction: A National Trend Moves into the Rocky Mountain Region. Symposium presented at the meeting of the Rocky Mountain Psychological Association, Denver, May 1971.

Sheppard, W.C. and MacDermot, H.G. Design and Evaluation of a Programmed Course in Introductory Psychology. *Journal of Applied Behavior Analysis,* 1970, *3,* 5-11.

David G. Born is with the Department of Psychology and **Steven Zlutnick** is with the Department of Psychiatry, University of Utah, Salt Lake City.

The Audio-Tutorial System: Incorporating Minicourses and Mastery

S.N. Postlethwait and Robert N. Hurst

A student can select four variations of coffee from an ordinary vending machine, but when he enters the classroom he may receive instruction identical to that of several hundred other students. It is an obvious fact of life that people exhibit great diversity in backgrounds, interests and capacities, yet our educational system is made up of large blocks of content (courses) with little or no provision to break the lockstep of time, content or instructional procedure. There is some justification for the classroom approach, however, since education is not just a dispensing procedure and the teacher is vital to the learning process. Many people can trace their excitement about a specific subject to the special way the subject was presented by a great teacher. Unfortunately these "great teachers" are rather rare, and physical limitations permit only a few students to "sit at their feet." While it is true that the talent of these teachers has been made available to some degree through their writings, many good teachers never write for publication, and even so, the limitation imposed by the printed word negates the potential of the teacher for the clever use of tangible objects and sound.

Hopkins has suggested that the best learning situation is the "teacher on one end of the log and the student on the other." Hopkins assumed the teacher was a "good" teacher and, if one can assume the log was figurative, the concept serves as a proper model for the Audio-Tutorial (AT) system. The AT system, used in conjunction with minicourses, while retaining compatability with the conventional educational system, has great potential for providing students with improved access to "good" teachers and with some other important features, such as greater individualization. This paper describes a pilot study currently being conducted at Purdue University.

History of the AT System

At Purdue University the senior author began an attempt to provide a remedial program in a freshman botany course in 1961. The initial effort involved the production of a weekly lecture on audio tape. This was soon expanded to include: (1) tangible objects (specimens, experimental equipment, models), (2) printed materials (texts, study guides, journal articles) and (3) projected images (slides and movies). Ultimately the program was produced by assembling the appropriate items ("logs") and, while sitting among these items, recording on audio tape the conversation one would expect to use with a single student while tutoring the student through a sequence of learning activities. The product, i.e., the tape and other materials, was then duplicated as many times as necessary to accommodate all students. Because of student enthusiasm for the program the procedure was expanded to cover the content for the entire botany course. The course was then restructured to include three major types of study sessions:

1. Independent Study Session (ISS). Audio-tutorial programs were placed in a learning center which was open from 7:30 A.M. to 10:30 P.M. Monday through Friday. The student could come in at his convenience and check into a booth. On his way to the booth he would pick up a mimeographed sheet of objectives written in behavioral terms. Other components needed to complete the program (except for the student's own copy of the textbook and study guide) were housed in the booth. Materials too bulky or too expensive to include in each booth were placed on a central table for common use by all students. The student placed the headphones in position and, by listening to the tape, he experienced a simulated one-to-one tutoring by the instructor (Figure 1). The student could pace his study as he desired, stopping at any point in the program to use additional resources such as supplemental texts and discussions with the instructor on

Figure 1

*A Typical AT Booth Arrangement Including a
Portion of the Materials for a Minicourse.*

duty or with peers. Each student proceeded independently of other students and was free to omit any part of the study that was unnecessary for him to achieve the stated objectives for the week. The prep room was equipped with a table, chairs and a coffee urn to encourage students to take frequent breaks and to enter into discussions with peers over a cup of coffee. When the student was satisfied with his progress he was free to leave without regard to scheduled class time.

2. General Assembly Session (GAS). This session was scheduled on a weekly basis and included 300 or more students. Activities in this assembly involved an occasional lecture, special films, major exams and other activities that could be done most effectively in a large group. Attendance was required only for certain special events.

3. Integrated Quiz Session (IQS). This session involved eight students and an instructor and was scheduled to meet weekly for one-half hour. The primary purpose of the session was to exploit the principle that "one really learns a subject when one is required to teach it." For this session each student was expected to prepare a little lecture about each of the items used in the ISS. The instructor presented the items in the sequence programmed earlier and selected the student to lecture on a random basis. Thus all students were forced to organize the subject matter in their own minds and could not rely on superficial responses to instructor questions. In addition, this session provided the following:

(1)   direct feedback on the effectiveness of the components of the AT program,

(2)   an opportunity for each student to know at least one instructor very well,

(3)   each student to be well known by at least one instructor, and

(4)   an opportunity to take care of certain administrative details.

The AT system in this form has been adopted in a great many schools and in a broad spectrum of disciplines. (One-third of the papers presented at the Second Annual Audio-Tutorial Conference held at Purdue in November 1970 dealt with subject matter areas outside the field of biology, and several were concerned with programs below the college level.) Obviously, the effectiveness of the AT system corresponds directly to the ability of the "good" teacher to prepare the AT programs and to originate the necessary supplementary sessions. Many teachers report highly successful systems.

Minicourses and Mastery. In 1969, when Robert N. Hurst joined the staff at Purdue University with the assignment to convert a zoology course (Biology 109) to the Audio-Tutorial approach, it was decided to reorganize the content of both the zoology and botany courses into smaller units of information called minicourses. Each minicourse would cover a reasonably coherent segment of subject matter (topic) and each minicourse would have a written set of specific objects suitable for testing the student's mastery of the concepts included. No rigid guidelines were established as to length or teaching strategy. Primarily, the limits of a minicourse were determined by good judgment, much as one decides on how to divide a book into chapters. Approximately 30 minicourses covered subjects common to both zoology and botany. It was clear that if students were required to master the objectives in their first study of the common minicourses it would be redundant to involve them with the same subject matter a second time in the subsequent course.

As each student mastered the objectives for a particular common minicourse, it was recorded on his individual card, and he was not required to repeat the minicourse study again. Thus, students entering the two-course sequence through either botany or zoology, and taking the common minicourses during their first enrollment, accumulated some time which could be devoted to the exploration of their own interests through the study of optional minicourses during the second semester of their enrollment. The botany and zoology courses which had previously been two distinct four-credit-hour courses now became a "pool" of minicourses divided into four categories, as follows:

1. Plant minicourses
2. Animal minicourses
3. Common minicourses
4. Optional minicourses

Students entering the botany-zoology complex by the way of botany were required to take the plant minicourses and common minicourses, and those students entering the complex by way of zoology were required to take the animal minicourses and common minicourses. Optional minicourses were selected by the student during the second semester of enrollment as needed to complete the requirement for the full four credit hours in botany and four credit hours in zoology.

Most of the objectives for each minicourse were written at the knowledge and comprehension level. When a student achieved mastery for a given minicourse, he had a C entered on his record for that minicourse. After completing the required number of minicourses at this level, the student was awarded a grade of C in the course for which he was enrolled. A student who had not completed the number of minicourses required for the course for which he was enrolled was given a grade of incomplete, with the opportunity to complete the uncompleted minicourses during the subsequent semester. At that time, the incomplete would be removed and a permanent grade would be assigned by the Registrar's office.

Students who wished to earn grades of A or B could do so by completing additional activities requiring a greater knowledge and "understanding" of science, a greater time input and more creative ability. The A-B activities were administered on a point basis. Students receiving an A were expected to acquire 110 points, while those working for a B had to acquire 85 points. These points were earned by participating in a variety of activities including special examinations, outside readings, research projects, peer tutoring activities, library projects and other activities agreed upon between the student and the instructor.

After two years' experience it is clear that it is possible to combine the Audio-Tutorial system with the concepts of mini-courses and mastery to develop a learning system which provides a great deal more individualization and flexibility than the conventional lecture-laboratory approach.

Some Advantages and Disadvantages

A partial list of the advantages of the AT-minicourse system is as follows:

1. The primary learning program can be prepared by a "good" teacher. All his skill in selecting and sequencing learning activities can be made available to each student on a simulated tutorial basis.

2. The rate and emphasis of study is directly under the student's control. He can stop at any point in the program to obtain outside assistance (instructor, peer, book or other resources). He can repeat or skip any segment of the program in accordance with his needs.

3. The system is designed for success. The expectation is that all students will achieve the objectives of each minicourse. The

relatively small units of subject matter are less forbidding than a complete course might be, and a sense of accomplishment is achieved with the mastery of each minicourse.

4. There is great flexibility for individualizing course content to the specific needs of students. Minicourses can be selected and combined in a variety of ways to accommodate major goals, interests, capacities and backgrounds.

5. Redundancy can be reduced, and efficient use of facilities, staff and student time can be achieved.

6. The media and instructional strategies used will reflect the creativity of the instructor, his facilities, the nature of the subject matter and the objectives selected for use.

7. Programs that involve primarily portable items could be made available outside the Learning Center. Perhaps several minicourses constituting a relatively high proportion of a regular course could be studied at home, and thus reduce the cost to both the student and the school.

8. The transfer of materials between courses and between institutions could be accomplished more readily because each minicourse is essentially an independent learning system and could be easily combined with others to adapt to the local situation.

A partial list of the disadvantages of the AT-minicourse system is as follows:

1. The development and testing of an AT-minicourse program is time consuming and requires considerable skill and talent.

2. The system requires psychological adjustment for both student and teacher. The student must assume a greater degree of responsibility for his own progress and make some decisions for himself. The teacher must become committed to "helping students learn" and be willing to accept less attention to himself and his role in the learning process. Further, the teacher must adjust to having all his efforts and objectives exposed to students and colleagues for review and criticism.

3. Many factors only tangentially related to the system may frustrate and create unexpected difficulties which have undue influence on the success of the program. A change from the routine within routine surroundings is never easy.

Summary

Although the pilot study using the AT system with mini-courses and mastery concepts has been underway only three years, it is apparent that it is feasible and practical even in a conventional university setting. Its potential for individualization is well received by students, and the administration of the program can be accomplished by redeploying about the same number of staff as required for conventional teaching.

The authors' hopes for their botany and zoology students have nearly all been realized. Perhaps more important, however, is the potential of the minicourse concept for providing new ways of "going to college" and for assisting with equal opportunity education and continuing education. Alternatives to the existing educational system are necessary to accommodate the needs of a substantial portion of the population. Many of these people are unable to fit into the traditional regimen of "going to school" for a variety of reasons, but they still have the desire to and need for expanding their education. Self-instructional minicourses in the format described in this paper can provide the necessary flexibility and portability with no compromise in the quality of instruction. The compatibility of the system with conventional procedures makes it feasible to intermix the two approaches with no loss or problem to the student. The major task obviously is to produce the quantity and quality of minicourses necessary to accommodate current needs, and to devise the additional administrative procedures required to make such programs available on a broad scale.

S.N. **Postlethwait** and **Robert N. Hurst** are members of the Department of Biological Sciences, Purdue University, Lafayette, Indiana.

The COMPAC:
An Instructional Package
for Competency-Based
Teacher Education

William M. Bechtol

Southwest Minnesota State College is new. Five years ago the spot where the College now stands was a cornfield. Today this cornfield has been transformed into modern structures designed to educate students in new, exciting and promising ways. In June 1971, the Charter Class graduated from Southwest. One group of these students had a unique educational experience. They are the first graduates of a competency-based teacher education program. This chapter focuses on this program and the instructional packages that have been developed to achieve it.

In developing this program, the staff of the Division of Education explored the question, "What does a teacher need to know and be able to do?" As they sought answers from teachers, public school administrators, trainers of teachers, state department of education personnel and researchers in education, the key idea that emerged was the concept of competency-based teacher education.

It appeared obvious that if the aim of teaching is learning, there should be evidence that pre-service teachers can bring about appropriate learning in students before they assume responsibility for such learning in the classroom. The development of a teacher education program that generates this kind of evidence is mandatory.

While developing a competency-based teacher education program, several tasks were identified. The pupil outcomes that are desired (the goals of education) must be identified. The conditions which bring about the desired pupil outcomes (the instruction program within the schools) must be identified. In developing this program the Southwest Minnesota State College Education Division staff found that competency-based teacher education must also be field-centered, individualized and systematically designed. These were new concepts. The idea that teacher certification be based upon tested teaching competencies rather than courses was revolutionary. The idea that these competencies must be tested within the public schools made the program field-centered and at the same time recognized the partnership between public schools and colleges for training pre-service teachers. It became obvious to the staff in planning this program that it must be individualized; as a matter of fact, the teacher education program began to model what the individualized school program would look like. The design of teacher education was also an important concept. This design had to be purposeful, data dependent and adaptive. With these concepts in mind the Southwest Teacher Education Program was organized.

The traditional plan of separating elementary and secondary education did not seem appropriate for a competency-based program. Many of the competencies required by elementary and secondary teachers are the same. The abrupt division between these two programs seemed to be quite artificial to the planning staff. Consequently, three learning and research centers were organized within the Division of Education to help a student develop necessary competencies for certification.

Each of the three centers has specific responsibilities for developing teacher competencies. The Center for Educational Studies is responsible for developing curriculum packages and instructing students in educational psychology, child and adolescent growth and development, learning theory and evaluation. The Center for Management of Educational Systems is responsible for developing curriculum packages and instructing students in classroom management, school organization, curriculum development and the selection of appropriate content, materials and instructional strategies. The Center for Applied Instruction provides the student field experiences so that he can observe, practice, test and finally develop specific teaching competencies. Time for the pre-service teacher to work in the public schools to observe, to microteach and to student teach is provided by this center.

A key step in the development of this program was the acceptance of a model for instructional management. This model provided a plan for organizing the curriculum for the teacher education program; for teaching these competencies; and for the teacher to use once he is employed in the public school (see Figure 1).

The model was used for organizing the curriculum for teacher education. The model helped identify what a teacher needed to be able to do. The teacher needed (1) competencies in specifying educational objectives which reflect issues relevant to education and to living in our modern-day democracy, (2) competencies in determining conditions of the learner in relation to the specified objectives, (3) competencies in selecting, preparing and using appropriate materials, activities and reinforcements for the learner, (4) competencies in organizing and managing the variety of learning environments which promote individualized instruction and (5) competencies in evaluation procedures to determine whether mastery of the educational objectives has been achieved.

The teacher education curriculum is organized into competency packages (ComPacs) which are classified according to the five steps of the model (i.e., those ComPacs on Specifying Objectives are classified 1.0; those on Determining the Condition of the Learner are classified 2.0; etc.). This classification system corresponded to the requirements of a computer-managed program which began in the 1971-72 school year. The ComPacs are modeled after the UNIPAC which was developed by I/D/E/A, a subsidiary of the Kettering Foundation (see the Feild-Swenson paper in this book). The individualized competency packages contain the five steps of the model and in reality are a prototype of the model in action. Students select ComPacs and work on them at their own speed in an individualized program.

The ComPacs contain behavioral objectives that are sequenced from knowledge to application. Almost all ComPac sequences end with the pre-service teacher applying his new knowledge with students in the public school as a part of the field

Figure 1

Instructional Management

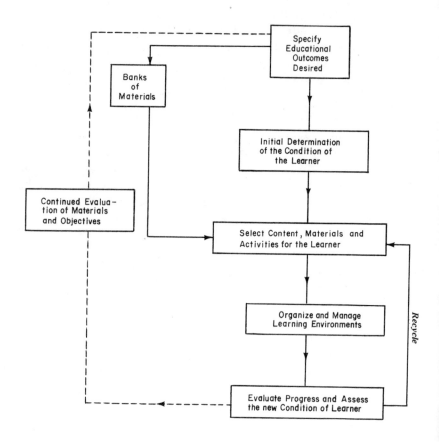

experience activities.

Figure 2 shows ComPac 1.0111, which is the first ComPac in the behavioral objective sequence. After completion of this ComPac the student should be able to recognize and write behavioral objectives. Compac 1.0112 teaches a student to write behavioral objectives in the cognitive, affective and psychomotor domains. ComPac 1.0113 is a field task; the learner develops a behavioral objective (or sequence) for a pupil who is having learning problems. After completion of ComPac 1.0114 the student is able to successfully microteach a behavioral objective to a group of students. One can see how ComPacs are sequenced and how they are designed to permit students to demonstrate competencies.

Figure 2

Southwest Minnesota State College
Marshall, Minnesota

Compac 1.0111	Stating Objectives in Behavioral Terms
CONTEXT:	Specify Educational Outcomes Desired
MAJOR SUBJECT:	Educational Objectives
TOPIC:	Stating Objectives in Behavioral Terms
TARGET POPULATION:	Pre-Service Elementary and Secondary, In-Service

BEHAVIORAL OBJECTIVES:

1. Given a set of objectives, the student will select those that are measurable objectives by identifying in each given objective the following elements:
    a. A statement of the task the student will perform.
    b. A description of the conditions under which the student will be required to perform the task.
    c. The acceptable level of performance.

2. Given a description of teaching tasks and sources of information, the student will write measurable behavioral objectives.

PREREQUISITE: None required

PRETEST: None for pre-service teachers

For In-Service Teachers who are familiar with the concepts of behavioral objectives, an evaluator will conduct an interview with the learner before this ComPac is begun. If the evaluator feels that the learner understands the area covered in this ComPac, he will instruct the student to take the self-test on pages 56-60 of *Preparing Instructional Objectives* by Robert F. Mager. If the learner misses five or fewer on this test, he may exit this ComPac.

Objective One: Identifying Behavioral Objectives

1. Read: *Preparing Instructional Objectives* by Robert F. Mager.

2. View: the filmstrip-cassette set "Systematic Instructional Decision-Making" (VIMCET No. 55). Write the answer as you view.

3. View: "Educational Objectives" (VIMCET No. 54). Write the answer as you view.

4. Read: William, Ragan. *Modern Elementary Curriculum,* pages 113-125, "Nature and Function of Educational Objectives."

ALTERNATE PLAN: With an overhead projector, view transparency set on Behavioral Objectives available in the lab.

Objective Two: Initial Practice in Writing Behavioral Objectives

ELEMENTARY:
1. Write five behavioral objectives for the following teaching situations:
    a. Teaching directions on a wall map.
    b. Teaching kindergarten children to identify five colors.
    c. Teaching primary children to regroup (borrow) in subtraction.

SECONDARY:
1. Write five behavioral objectives in your own discipline.

EVALUATION:

After you have written five behavioral objectives, show your written objectives to a faculty member (CMES).

MATERIALS:

Mager, Robert F. *Preparing Instructional Objectives,* Fearon Publishers, Palo Alto, California, 1962.

Ragan, William. *Modern Elementary Curriculum,* Holt, Rinehart and Winston, New York, 1966.

Filmstrip viewer and cassette recorder

"Systematic Instructional Decision-Making" (VIMCET No. 55)—filmstrip-cassette set

"Instructional Objectives" (VIMCET No. 54)—filmstrip-cassette set

Overhead projector and Behavioral Objectives transparencies

QUEST: To be initiated by learner

In deciding which competencies a teacher needs, the staff had to predict the kind of school we will have or should have in the future. The ComPacs are designed to provide a pre-service or in-service teacher with the required competencies to teach in the individually guided instruction program of a multi-unit elementary school. This school organization pattern accepts the concepts of non-grading, team teaching, multi-age grouping, continuous progress curricula, differentiated staffing and individualized instruction. The model is adaptable to the needs of students and those of the community where it is located. It appeared to the Southwest staff that this organization provided an appropriate model for training elementary teachers for the 1970s and 1980s. Southwest faculty teaches in the same manner as the faculty of a multi-unit elementary school. In this way pre-service elementary teachers not only study so that they can assume a role in individually guided education, they also become students in such a system.

Perhaps the strongest part of the program is the modeling. The Southwest faculty models and demonstrates how a teacher works with students in an individualized program. Consequently, pre-service and in-service teachers use ComPacs and individualized instruction techniques in their own classroom.

One can perhaps better understand the Southwest Teacher Education Program by following a pre-service elementary teacher through the program. A student does not enter the teacher education program until his junior year. By the time he enters the program he has successfully completed two years of a liberal arts education. At this time the student applies for admission to the teacher education program. The criteria for admission are (1) success in academic disciplines, (2) demonstrated ability to utilize American language and communications skills, (3) good physical health and (4) a recommendation by his advisor that the candidate has coped successfully with personal and social problems and is ready to work with students in a public school.

Once the pre-service teacher is accepted into the teacher education program, he enrolls in Elementary Block I. This is the first of five blocks (each gives six quarter-hours credit) in which he will enroll. The flexible concept of a block rather than a course permits an instructor to develop an individually guided education program for each pre-service elementary teacher.

Block I is the orientation to education and to an individual-ized program. Research has shown that it is necessary for pre-service teachers to focus on themselves first before they can really reach out and care about others; hence, it is necessary for pre-service teachers to have a series of human relations exercises and to see themselves in a school setting so they can determine what skills, knowledge and competencies they need to be a teacher. The individually guided education program is a new experience for many students. Students need help, direction and encouragement to work in such a program. Their advisor in Block I helps them become independent learners.

The advisory group is one of the most effective and innovative aspects of the Teacher Education Program. Once a student enrolls in Elementary Block I, he is assigned to an advisory group of 15-20 students. The instructor of this group becomes this student's advisor. The student is assigned to this advisory group for five elementary blocks. This organization gives the student and his advisor a chance to know each other well. It provides a peer group of other students who are studying to become elementary teachers. The advisory group begins with a number of human relations activities so that the members get to know and become more open with each other. The group becomes supportive so that simulation, value clarification and microteaching activities can be attempted. Core groups or sub-groups within an advisory group give students experiences in planning, interacting and completing tasks similar to those that members of a teaching team experience. Core groups are assigned to the same schools as teams for initial field experiences.

All students enrolled in Blocks 2-3-4-5 attend a common, one-hour large group session once each week. This plan models multi-age grouping. Some students have completed just one block. Others have student-taught. They attend advisory groups once each week. It is here that personalized contracts to achieve teacher competencies are developed. Final contracts are written in one-to-one conferences with the advisor and advisee. Students choose to do ComPacs, attend seminars, work directly in schools, microteach or do independent research to achieve teaching competencies.

As an alternate learning plan, a comprehensive seminar schedule is developed each week. Students have the option of attending seminars to achieve specific competencies. Seminars are led by education professors, public school personnel, other college personnel and education students. Competencies achieved through performance in seminars are also coded and placed in the computer-managed student files.

Much of a student's time is spent working on competency packages. An extensive educational laboratory to house ComPacs and support materials has been organized. A student works on ComPacs in the education laboratory, the library, his own room and the public school. Some ComPacs are required; others are student choices. Students work on ComPacs on their own time and at their own pace. Most ComPacs end with one-to-one evaluation between a professor and the student. Professors are assigned to the education laboratory six hours per week to evaluate students. Personalized learning truly occurs during these one-to-one evaluation sessions.

The favorite activity of the pre-service teachers during the elementary blocks is the field experience. Students work in the public schools one-half day per week. They work as teaching assistants to help the school program; they also work on ComPacs for the public school program. Many of the students are "turned on" by this experience. They voluntarily work many hours in the school—preparing materials, tutoring, supervising students, correcting tests or even teaching as members of a team.

After the completion of three elementary blocks, the student may apply for student teaching. The criteria for student teachers are (1) academic standing, (2) completion of three or more elementary blocks, (3) successful field experiences in the public school and (4) recommendation of advisor.

ComPacs contain knowledge objectives which can be learned at the College and application objectives which must be learned in the classroom. The pre-service teacher must demonstrate teaching competencies with pupils. To achieve a competency-based curriculum such as this, the Division of Education had the choice of staffing a laboratory school or developing a good working relationship with the schools of the area. Working with area schools was congruent with the mission of the College; consequently, a decision was made that these objectives could be met best in the public schools by means of the "teacher education center" concept.

The teacher education center approach had been developed and tested at the University of Maryland. This concept is a unified approach to the study of teaching and supervision. It is a coordinated program of pre-service and in-service experiences planned and administered cooperatively by a college and the public schools. The program is designed to serve the needs and interests of the experienced professional as well as those of the inexperienced undergraduate student. An individualized approach makes it possible for each to become a student of teaching in accordance with his own particular stage of professional development. Organizationally, the teacher education centers in Southwest Minnesota have been five school districts. Coordinating the continuing career development program in each center is a teacher education coordinator who was jointly selected and employed by the College and the public school. His role is to plan an effective program of laboratory experiences for the college student assigned to the center schools and to coordinate an in-service program for the center staffs (these are the regular teachers of the school district who work with these students).

The teacher education center approach comes from the mutual desire on the part of the College and the public schools to develop a more effective teacher education program. New commitment from both is required for the center to succeed. The public school must assume an increased and continuing responsibility for pre-service training. The college must assume an increased and continuing responsibility for in-service training.

Pre-service teachers are assigned to centers for junior year field experiences and for student teaching. A student teacher is assigned to the teaching center as part of the instructional team. He is not assigned to an individual teacher. This gives him the opportunity to associate and work with many faculty members. The student teacher assumes instructional responsibility for some specific aspects of the curriculum. He also demonstrates specific teaching competencies. The center coordinator individualizes each student teaching experience, using a wide variety of intensive and extensive experiences geared to meet the needs of the particular student. Each Center is equipped with video equipment for microteaching and for recording classroom performance. Weekly seminars are led by the teaching center coordinator to personalize and to evaluate the teaching experiences for each student teacher assigned to his center.

After the student completes the student teaching component, he returns to the college for a final evaluation. A student's graduation and certification is dependent upon demonstrated teaching competencies. These competencies include knowing what to teach, pre-assessment skills, selecting appropriate materials, choosing effective instructional strategies, and evaluation skills. Students demonstrate these competencies by completing Com-Pacs, microteaching, conducting small groups and actually teaching in the public schools.

Plans are made to follow-up the charter class teachers and to evaluate the effectiveness of each ComPac. The ComPac may provide a model for other teacher training institutions that are implementing competency-based teacher education. Many believe that the Southwest program is a hopeful solution to the complex problems of preparing competent teachers for individually guided education.

William M. Bechtol is Director, Center for Management of Educational Systems, Southwest Minnesota State College, Marshall.

The Structure and Substance of the WILKIT Instructional Module

Caseel D. Burke

WILKITs (Weber Individualized Learning Kits) are a product of the teacher education faculty at Weber State College, and are developed and used within the context of a system identified as the Individualized, Performance-Based Teacher Education Program (IPT), which has been in operation since September, 1970. Motivation for development of the system of WILKITs came from the reaction of the faculty against the sterile and unstimulating lecture procedures which the WILKITs replaced.

The WILKIT is a unit of work intended to assist a student in the professional component of teacher education toward mastery of an educational concept or a teaching skill, process or strategy. A WILKIT is a delivery system for a single part of the teacher preparation program. Related WILKITs are grouped into course blocks and related course blocks are organized into systems for preparing elementary and secondary school teachers (see Appendices A and B).

The Objective of a System

Basic to the development of a system of teacher education is a clearly defined statement of purpose. The following are identified as the assumptions (beliefs, guidelines, aims, goals, objectives, etc.) of those who developed the IPT and the WILKITs:

A good teacher education system:
1. derives its substance and standards from the nature and needs of successful teaching.

2. exists on the merits of its accomplishments.
3. attracts the respect of scholarly college students and faculty.
4. demonstrates a variety of effective teaching models.
5. provides for the individual abilities and needs of its students and faculty.
6. provides human relations training.
7. fosters the qualities of initiative, judgment and responsibility.
8. is flexible, adaptable and sensitive to the need for change.
9. demonstrates theory in practice.
10. makes extensive use of meaningful field experiences.
11. takes advantage of technological aids to learning.
12. is a shared responsibility of the total educational system.

The Substance of Teacher Education

A task analysis of the work of the teacher is the usual procedure for determining the content of teacher preparation. Such analyses have identified hundreds of individual teaching skills or tasks that presumably should be studied or mastered by the student. Being aware of such studies and at the same time being faced with the practical problem of building and putting into operation an individualized, performance-based system, the teacher education faculty at Weber State College chose to chart a course based on their own combined judgment and including as many useful ideas as they could glean from other sources. They had confidence in much of the content of teacher education they had been dealing with and they felt there was value in working the ground which was familiar to them.

Each faculty member accepted the task of thoroughly analyzing the courses he or she taught and of identifying those topics considered vital to teacher preparation. At this point an advisory committee, consisting of sixteen public school teachers, administrators and college students, met periodically with the faculty to provide input on the selection of the content. Final decisions on what topics to include, and in what sequence and relationship, rested with the faculty. The content of the IPT system, after all the adjustments and decisions were made, consisted of a tentative list of approximately seventy topics considered vital to professional teacher education. For each one of these topics, a self-instructional unit (WILKIT) has been developed and is in use. Expansion of the system to include various kinds of special education presumes the development of additional WIL-KITs to meet such specific needs. The following are typical of the topics selected for basic teacher preparation:

Lesson and Unit Planning	Classroom Management and Discipline
Growth and Development	Transfer of Learning
Principles of Reinforcement	Self-Concept
Group Processes	Motivation and Learning
Purposes and Methods of Classroom Evaluation	Reading Study Techniques
Student Record and Referral Services	Phonic Analysis Skills
Tutoring Techniques	Written Communication
Media Production—Transparencies	Music for Children
Media Equipment Operation—Overhead Projectors	Classroom Strategies—Individualization

The Weber teacher education faculty has long emphasized the similarities rather than the differences in teaching at the elementary and secondary levels. Thus, mutual and cooperative planning between the two departments was natural and unforced. Many WILKITs are used for preparing both elementary and secondary candidates. Some, as observed from the above list, are specialized toward one or the other level.

The WILKIT Format

The length of the WILKIT learning module varies in adjusting to such considerations as the importance of the topic, the nature of the learning experiences and the student response. Length is subject to modification as need dictates. Student clock-time needed to complete a WILKIT varies from module to module. The overall range is from about ten to forty clock-hours. The estimated time required is stated at the beginning of each module. In completing a particular WILKIT, the time spent varies considerably from student to student.

The WILKITs are developed within a general pattern. Each one ordinarily has the following elements:

Title	— identifies the topic
Introduction	— provides a setting for the topic
Content	— states the problems or considerations to be dealt with
Pre-assessment	— helps the student know the level at which he can already perform
Behavioral Objectives	— identifies what behavior is sought and at what level of proficiency
Learning Experiences	— lists suggested or required learning experiences for meeting the behavioral objectives
Self-evaluation	— self-assesses the student's level of accomplishment
Proficiency Assessment	— determines if the behavioral objectives have been met

Experience in using the module shows that students soon get used to the pattern. This familiarity then helps in approaching subsequent WILKITs. Having variety in the length of units and keeping within a time range of about fifteen to forty clock-hours appear to be advantageous.

The WILKIT Structure

The pattern of each WILKIT, which identifies the behavioral criteria expected from study of the module, is consistent with the performance-based idea of teacher preparation. Learning experiences are provided which have been carefully selected to assist the student. It is assumed that on completion of these experiences he will be ready to pass the performance assessment. The assessment is designed to determine whether or not the behavioral criteria have been achieved. If the result is negative, a recycling through certain experiences is prescribed to produce the necessary outcomes. In student teaching the application of the acquired performance takes place. The developmental pattern of the system is illustrated as follows:

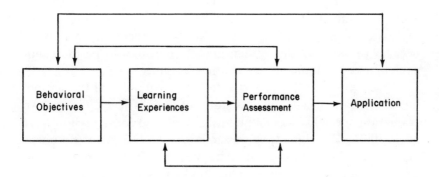

Assuming the objectives are authentic and the application is accomplished in student teaching, the system is functioning as planned. However, should certain objectives fail to appear in the behavior of the student teacher, one of two things may be suspected. Either the objectives are unnecessary in teaching or they have not been learned effectively. Thus, it is evident that accountability is vital in validating the structural pattern of the system.

Evaluation of Accountability

Although major decisions in developing the WILKIT module were made arbitrarily by the faculty, they were arrived at through careful study and deliberation. The faculty, with the help of students, the college administration, public school personnel and professional consultants, weighed each idea as the system evolved. Since the task was to develop and place in operation a system without benefit of a working model to follow, the developers were constantly confronted with the question, "How will this work in our situation?" This posed considerations such as the capabilities and limitations of the faculty, the reactions of students, the rigidity of college policies and the availability of learning resources as well as the general educational climate of the area.

It was the conclusion of the faculty, supported by the opinion of a number of consultants of national stature, that the basic concepts of the system were educationally sound. It was also accepted, generally, that the only way to test the worth of such a system is to try it in operation. The developers were agreed that thorough evaluation of the system at every step was crucial to its success as well as necessary to its survival. Accountability, then, became the key to the system and it continues to be the major guideline as development and testing continue.

Since the WILKITs constituted the focal point of the system, initial evaluation began with a study of their efficiency in use. An evaluation specialist was temporarily employed for the school year of 1970-71. His chief task was to promote and analyze student input for the purpose of determining WILKIT results and consequent needed changes. One kind of student reaction was a simple evaluation form filled out and deposited with the operations office as each WILKIT was completed. Personal interviews with students by faculty members also produced numerous suggestions and criticisms. Analyses of the written reactions have been made available periodically to the individual faculty members concerned and, after the first year of operation, almost every WILKIT has been revised on the basis of needs discovered by the students and faculty. During the first few weeks of operation, abrupt adjustments were effected in certain WILKITs due to identification of such things as discrepancies in amount of work required or in the overall balance being sought in the system.

The most common kinds of changes made in the first revision of the WILKITs were those dealing with (1) clarification of instructions to the student and (2) adding or deleting learning experiences and materials. Some adjustments in the placement of WILKITs within credit blocks has also been accomplished.

The responsibility taken by students in providing their reactions to the WILKITs in constructive ways is worthy of note. Many hundreds of responses have been made, both written and oral. Practically all of these have been in the form of constructive suggestions. To the credit of the faculty is the fact that response to student reaction has been prompt and meaningful. The process has developed an attitude of mutual responsibility on the part of students and faculty for improving the system. Evaluation of the WILKITs as teaching-learning instruments is a continuous process. It is anticipated new and additional means will be developed to make this process more effective.

An evaluative instrument was developed to determine the extent to which the processes learned in the WILKITs are being demonstrated in student teaching. This aid to observation and evaluation was field tested during the 1971-72 school year. Further use of the instrument is anticipated in working with first-year teachers in local school districts under a federal- and state-sponsored EPDA project entitled Resident Initiatory Teaching Experience (RITE). The ultimate effort to evaluate the WILKIT delivery system will be to determine what is happening to children under teachers who have prepared under this system. Further planning is underway for this purpose.

Operation of the System

When a student registers for a professional course, such as Education 340, Instructional Skills for Secondary Teachers, for six quarter-hours of credit, he receives the eight WILKITs that comprise that course. A fee of $1.25 for each WILKIT is required to cover costs of the unit and the supporting instructional materials. As each WILKIT is completed, the faculty member in charge certifies this fact to the operations center. As the course block is finished, a grade of "pass" is sent to the office of the registrar. If the credit block is not completed within the quarter, an "incomplete" is turned in. This may be changed to "pass" within a year.

Extensive materials and equipment support the learning experiences involved in the units. The student has use of a special collection of multiple reading sources prescribed in the WILKITs and available on two-day reserve in the College Library. He also has use of the dial access system of the Library for many of the audio, video and film resources prescribed in the units. The learning materials center is available for the development of teaching aids and for practice in the use of equipment. At the operations center the student obtains WILKITs, takes final written assessments, schedules faculty interviews and seminars and arranges for group sessions, microteaching and other WILKIT activities.

Within close proximity to the College are numerous public schools of high quality where students engage in laboratory experiences required in the WILKITs. All visits to the schools are arranged through the office of the director of laboratory experiences.

Student and Faculty Roles

Through financial assistance from the Carnegie Corporation of New York, the faculty members gained nearly the equivalent of a school year of released time from their teaching assignments to engage in curriculum development. Substitute faculty members capably conducted most of the coursework in the ongoing program. The tremendous task of developing the instructional units would have taken an estimated five to ten years without the released time provided.

Use of the WILKIT module has introduced new roles and relationships between student and faculty. With the elimination of regular classes the faculty have become advisors, counselors and consultants to the students. Since this pattern is new to both students and faculty, some problems of adjustment have arisen.

Many students are reluctant to arrange personal visits with faculty members. Failure to reserve time for professional study has caused conflicts of priority with regularly scheduled classes in other fields. Faculty members are not always available at the time students want to arrange interviews. Faculty members have had to learn how to balance their time equitably between advising students, conducting seminars, revising WILKITs, supervising student teachers and performing the innumerable tasks associated with conducting a new and developing system.

Students being responsible for their own progress places on them the burden of determining when they will study, how and in what setting it will be done and when assessment of progress will be accomplished. To meet the task requires careful planning and considerable self-discipline. Consequently, an unusually large number of incompletes were given during the first quarter or two. This situation began to clear up as more and more students moved ahead in the system.

Some Tentative Observations

The WILKIT module has been in use for the past two years as the basic teaching-learning unit of a total system of professional preparation for elementary and secondary school teachers. Since a thorough evaluation of the modules and the total system has been impossible at this early date, only tentative statements can be made as to the effectiveness of this particular instructional unit. From the observations and reactions of students, faculty and others who have studied the system, it appears evident that a major strength lies in the clearly defined objectives and stated levels of performance. Students claim to work harder and learn more from this initiative and responsibility on the part of students. The students react responsibly to a partnership with the faculty in attempting to improve the system. The academically capable students seem to have more success in the system and to accept it more readily than do the less capable students.

The faculty regards the present system as superior to the former in preparing teachers. Greater opportunity is provided for using faculty strengths to advantage. Differentiated staffing becomes more realistic. Faculty members adjust readily to their new roles as advisors and consultants to the students, and relations between students and faculty are more friendly and cooperative. In addition, strong encouragement has come from the Utah State Board of Education, and considerable enthusiasm for the system has been expressed among public school teachers and administrators.

APPENDIX A

Professional Course Requirements for Elementary School Teachers

September, 1971

                                                                    Quarter Hours

Education 195,*   Introductory Field Experience   1
   WILKIT: Orientation (W-3)

Education 300,   Fundamental Skills for Teachers   3
   WILKIT: Self-Concept (W-12)

Education 324,   Basic Skills for Elementary
                    Teachers   4
   WILKITS:
   W-57   Tutoring Techniques
   W-26   Reading Study Techniques
   W-35   Handwriting
   W-70   Media Equipment Operation
   W-14   School Health
   W-5   Growth and Development (May be waived
           upon successful completion of Family
           Life 150)

Education 325,   Elementary School Curriculum I   6
   WILKITS:
   W-27   Reading Readiness

*A "pre-professional" requirement

W-28   Nature and Instructional Implications
of Reading
W-29   Reading Comprehension
W-30   Basal Approach to Teaching Reading
W-31   Phonic Analysis Skills
W-32   Structural Analysis Skills
W-33   Dictionary Skills
W-36   Spelling
W-38   Oral and Written Communication

Education 326,   Elementary School Curriculum II   6
WILKITS:
W-6   Elementary School Mathematics I
W-9   Elementary School Mathematics II
W-42   Inquiry in Elementary Science
W-43   Organizing and Planning for Teaching
Elementary Science
W-50   Social Studies in the Elementary
Schools
W-54   Elementary Social Studies Instruction
W-40   Music for Children

Education 360,   Instructional Skills for Elementary
Teachers
WILKITS:
W-7   Principles of Reinforcement
W-20   Instructional Resources: Evaluation and
Use of Instructional Media
W-60   Media Production
W-22   Purposes and Methods of Evaluation
W-19   Professional Responsibilities
W-37   Listening
W-23   Art (May be waived upon successful
completion of Art 250)
W-39   The Language of Music (May be waived
upon successful completion of Music
320)

Education 488,   Teaching Practicum in Elementary
Education   15
WILKITS:
W-4   Classroom Management
W-13   Motivation and Learning

W-21   Classroom Group Meetings
W-10   Teaching and Learning in the
        Three Domains

Education 498,   Synthesis of the Elementary Teaching
                   Program   4
    WILKITS:
    W-8   Transfer of Learning
    W-16   Backgrounds of Educational Practice
    W-17   Professional Relationships
    W-18   Professional Rights

    Leadership or Service Practicum
    Prescribed Remediation or Optional WILKITS

                                   Total Professional   43

APPENDIX B

Professional Course Requirements for Secondary School Teachers

September, 1971

		Quarter Hours

Education 195,*   Introductory Field Experience   1
    WILKIT: Orientation (W-3)

Education 300,   Fundamental Skills for Teachers   3
    WILKIT: Self-Concept (W-12)

Education 350,   Theoretical Foundations of
                    Secondary Education   4
    WILKITS:
    W-57   Tutorial Techniques and Student
            Records

*A "pre-professional" requirement

W-5	Growth and Development Through Adolescence	
W-7	Principles of Reinforcement	
W-14	School Health	
W-55	Evaluating Teacher Behavior	

| Education 355, | Instructional Skills for Secondary Teachers | 6 |

WILKITS:

W-1	The Four Cs of Teaching
W-2	Lesson and Unit Planning
W-80	through 85, Options—Classroom Strategies
W-22	Purposes and Methods of Classroom Evaluation
W-20	Instructional Resources: Evaluation and Use of Instructional Media
W-60	Media Production
W-70	Media Equipment Operation

| Education 495, | Teaching Practicum in Secondary Education Student Teaching | 15 |

WILKITS:

W-10	Teaching and Learning in the Three Domains
W-4	Classroom Management
W-13	Motivation and Learning
W-21	Classroom Group Meetings

| Education 499, | Synthesis of the Secondary Teaching Program | 5 |

WILKITS:

W-11	Educational Research and the Teacher
W-18	Professional Rights
W-17	Professional Relationships
W-19	Professional Responsibilities
W-16	Backgrounds of Education Practice
W-8	Transfer of Learning

Leadership or Service Practicum
Prescribed Remediation or Optional WILKITS

Total Professional 34

Caseel D. Burke is Dean, School of Education, Weber State College, Ogden, Utah.

Training Packages: An Innovative Approach for Increasing IMC/RMC Potential for In-Service Training in Special Education

Dale D. Baum and Thomas G. Chastain

During its relatively short period of existence the Instructional Materials Center/Regional Media Center (IMC/RMC) Network has become increasingly aware that *providing* additional instructional materials to special education teachers does not necessarily guarantee efficient or effective use of them. The constant flow of requests from all levels of the educational community for continued training is a constant reminder to the Network that it must go far beyond the simplistic role of acquisition and dissemination of instructional materials.

All regional centers and many associate centers have tried to respond to the numerous requests for training teachers to become more proficient at recognizing and specifying learning problems, at evaluating and determining materials and methods to be used with specific problems, and to become more systematic in determining changes for children for whom learning is excessively difficult and problematic. Experience indicates, however, that Network personnel working singly in their respective service areas are too few to provide all the training that is requested and needed. Ironically perhaps, relief does not appear to be imminent from many colleges and universities.

Traditionally, teacher training institutions have encouraged their students to state objectives in the development of daily, weekly or longer lesson plans. The generality of this approach typically leads to stating global and vague instructional objectives such as "to understand," "to be aware of," "to appreciate," etc. Teacher training institutions, in general, tried to promulgate this behavior by stating or implying only very global objectives in their classes. While this approach to training teachers may be feasible for working with some pupils, it is often not a functional approach for dealing with children with exceptionalities or learning disabilities or with children experiencing even temporary learning problems. Beginning teachers who are generally lacking development in those skills considered essential for effective teaching continue to appear in classrooms (Hall, Panyan, Rabon and Broden, 1968). This would indicate that the results of valid research and/or innovations are not being successfully translated for implementation by teachers or for teachers at the college and university levels.

Training practicing teachers in the specific uses of new materials and the application of management, remedial and innovative teaching techniques places a severe demand on the personal resources of regional centers. A method for increasing the training potential of each regional center, representing an IMC/ RMC Network cooperative effort, would seem to constitute a reasonable step toward upgrading practicing teacher effectiveness through training. The proposed system for accomplishing this includes the development of "training packages."

Training Package

A "training package" is broadly conceived as a self-contained unit which may be delivered to associate centers or other locations and presented by local personnel with minimal effort and with maximum efficiency. The development of such packages would necessarily represent a union of the technology of hardware or machines (e.g., media) and technology adopted from the behavioral sciences (e.g., programming, feedback) culminating in an instructional technology and capability for training more teachers in the development of specific teaching and teaching related skills than is presently possible. The "training package" concept has the potential for multiplying many times the communication and training capabilities of the present staffs of the centers comprising the IMC/RMC Network.

In the foreword to the book *Preparing Instructional Objec-*

tives, Mager (1962) posed three questions which purportedly must be answered in order to instruct effectively:
(1)   What is it that we must teach?
(2)   How will we know when we have taught?
(3)   What materials and procedures will work best to teach what we wish to teach?

It is the thesis of Mager's book that these questions must be answered fully and in the order in which they are presented above, if instruction is to proceed effectively and efficiently. This procedure and adaptations of it are probably employed to some extent by a number of teachers with their pupils. There is, however, little evidence to support the notion that teachers in general practice the specificity demanded by this approach in their daily teaching. One explanation may lie in the possibility that teachers have never been taught by instructors who both advocated and practiced instructional objective specificity themselves.

It is proposed that the above three questions, when restated in the context of "training packages," serve as basic guidelines in the development of such packages for use with practicing special education teachers. In this context the questions would be stated as follows:
(1)   What shall we package for the special education teacher?
(2)   How will we know when a package is both efficient and effective?
(3)   Which formats and technologies will best present and communicate that which is to be taught?

What Shall We Package for the Special Education Teacher?

The answers to this multi-faceted question can initially be narrowed to two basic considerations. First, the teaching and teaching-related skills which many teachers need—but do not have—must be identified. The identification process can involve self-reporting by teachers as well as the observations of directors or supervisors of special education classes and programs. The observations of psychologists, resource or visiting teachers and principals would also be of value. It would be anticipated that initial responses from these populations would be rather broad and perhaps vague from an operational point of view, but nonetheless of value in determining both the content and priority for packaging.

The second consideration entails identifying within the professional community those teaching and teaching-related skills which have been demonstrated to be effective, but which have not been communicated in a useful way to practicing teachers. Much, if not all, that has been developed in education has been disseminated by way of professional publications and lectures. Current practices in education, however, indicate that these methods of communicating with teachers do not necessarily stimulate changes in teacher behavior for a variety of reasons. Therefore, it would be appropriate to consider innovative university and college training programs, the professional literature, demonstration projects, IMC/RMC training personnel, research and development centers and other professional personnel and organizations as potentially rich sources of teaching strategies and skills which could possibly be incorporated into training packages.

Both of the above considerations primarily involve identifying that which is needed and that which is or can be made available for packaging. With both sources of information available, a systematic and rational priority for packaging can be determined.

How Will We Know When a Package Is Both Efficient and Effective?

Training packages are developed to facilitate the attainment of the objectives of the package by specified populations. The training approach may be conceptualized as linear programming in the Skinnerian sense (Skinner, 1968) or as sequencing, as described by Bruner (1966). With these approaches, terminal skills or objectives are stated. Then a series of subskills are sequenced or programmed to facilitate attainment of the terminal objectives or skills.

Evaluation of packages is essentially evaluation of the training that occurs as a result of exposure to and interaction with the content of each package. The attainment of specific skills or behaviors may be monitored and measured by the use of pre- and posttests for both intermediate and terminal level skills. Self-evaluation by the target populations would be accomplished by programming appropriate feedback and knowledge of results systematically throughout the course of the package. The basic measure of the effectiveness of a package lies in its ability to guide the learning behaviors of teachers from a state of little or no skill to a state of learned and demonstrated skill within a specific content area designated by the objectives of the package.

The efficiency of the training potential of a package may be determined by comparing it with other methods of training, such as the traditional "pep talk" or "lecture-type" workshop. The variables which could be compared would include the levels of skill resulting from each method and the relative amounts of time and cost involved. It would be anticipated that the initial costs incurred in developing a single training package would far exceed the cost of engaging a speaking "expert" to present essentially the same material and skills to a group of teachers. However, the training package potential for continued re-use through multiple reproduction and nationwide dissemination through the IMC/RMC Network system may ultimately prove more efficient and effective than occasional presentations by experts.

Which Formats and Technologies Will Best Present and Communicate That Which Is To Be Taught?

As mentioned earlier, the development of training packages represents a union of the technology of hardware and the software technology adapted from the behavioral sciences. Past research generally supports the efficacy of programmed instruction for some pupils although the findings have not all been favorable. However, traditional teacher training, whether pre-service or in-service, has utilized the "lecture" approach almost exclusively. Therefore, there is little, if any, empirical evidence with which to answer the above question as it relates to the training of teachers.

It would be anticipated that the skills which are to be taught within a package approach would contribute to deciding which of the available technologies for formats would be utilized. Inherent in the package approach is active teacher involvement. The employment of technology by which actual cases or classroom settings can be simulated for training purposes can insure teacher involvement and practice in specific skill development. It would, however, be premature to make general statements regarding which formats or technologies should be employed with which contents. Rather, a more rational approach would be to decide upon the various technologies and formats in response to the demands of both questions one and two.

Training Package Examples

Training packages, as defined in this article, are not commercially available. There are, however, a few commercially available materials designed for both pre-service and in-service use which approach—to a limited extent—the packaging concept presented here. These include the Vimcet Filmstrip-Tape Programs (Popham and Baker, 1969) and Test Interpretation Kit I (McLarey and Bonk, 1968). Both these materials utilize filmstrips and audio tapes. Both materials are basically expository by design, although the Vimcet Programs do provide explicit instructional objectives, pre- and posttests and suggestions for practice activities. Both materials provide series of individual programs which can be presented singly in approximately one hour. This feature makes them particularly attractive for use during in-service training sessions held following the school day. It would appear that this design could be improved upon by programming adequate practice opportunities for skill development into each program.

In cooperation with the Rocky Mountain Special Education Instructional Materials Center and the Wyoming State Department of Special Education, the University of Kansas Special Education Instructional Materials Center developed a package for purposes of training primary level teachers in the diagnosis and remediation of reading problems. The package was designed in accordance with the rationale discussed previously. Throughout the package, reading was considered a behavioral response which could be observed, recorded and modified.

The major objectives of the package included the following:

(1) To train teachers to view reading from a behavioral point of reference.

(2) To train teachers to employ appropriate techniques for determining a child's reading level.

(3) To train teachers to identify a child's particular area of reading deficiency.

(4) To train teachers in the use of both formal and informal methods for locating appropriate reading materials.

(5) To train teachers to observe, record and graph reading responses in behavioral terms.

(6) To train teachers in the use of reinforcement contingencies in the teaching of reading.

In order to program for the attainment of the above objectives, a series of interrelated component-packages were developed, including (1) Informal Reading Diagnostic Techniques, (2) Diagnostic Tests of Phonics Skills, (3) Prescriptive Materials Retrieval System, (4) Informal Analysis of Materials, (5) Behavior Measurement and (6) Techniques of Reinforcement. Following the expository portion of each of the component-packages, training in each skill area was provided via simulated problems presented either visually or auditorily. All performance tasks were criterion-referenced, whereby each participant was expected to achieve at the 100 percent level from initial diagnosis through selecting appropriate materials to the development of prescriptive remedial programs of instruction.

A prototype of the package was presented to a group of 25 primary level teachers. Three two-day sessions were required to present the entire package. The two-day sessions were separated by two-week intervals, during which time the participants were instructed to implement the techniques previously taught and to collect appropriate data. These data, in conjunction with participant performance data collected during the presentations, provided a basis for package evaluation and subsequent modification. Also, the class performances of the 25 participants were monitored and evaluated during an entire school year for purposes of determining the effectiveness of the package content.

A unique feature in the training of the first 25 participants is that the participants were instructed in how to present the package to additional groups of teachers in their respective geographical regions. To date, the original 25 participants have used the package with an additional 150 primary level teachers. Both these teachers and their pupils will contribute valuable data for continued evaluation of the package format and its contents. These data will also be analyzed comparatively to determine the efficacy of utilizing teacher-participants to present the training package to their colleagues. In the more sparsely populated areas of the country, teacher potential as a multiplier for training other teachers via training packages seems especially worthy of investigation. The results of this investigation and the various evaluations discussed earlier will contribute to the final format of the contents of the package prior to its release to the Network.

Conclusion
Sharing between and among components of the Network has always been inherent in the IMC concept for both delivery of products and the communication of information and ideas. Instructional materials have served well as the vehicle for communicative development and exchange—particularly as they relate to associate or affiliate center development within the respective regions. It now appears that the evolving communications base can be both broadened and extended by capitalizing on the existing and potential training capabilities of the components comprising the IMC/RMC Network. This potential can only be realized, however, as each regional center becomes engaged in "packaging" its training efforts in such a manner that the training may be delivered to and shared with other regional and associate centers.

In this manner the training expertise of the nation can be harnessed, delivered and presented to local groups of teachers without undue delay. As each regional center becomes engaged in "packaging" activities, it would be anticipated that each would more closely monitor the demonstration projects, innovative programs, etc., within its region and possibly salvage valuable training material which otherwise might be diffused only through the pages of journals—which typically go unread by teachers. The training package concept, therefore, will enable regional centers to respond more adequately to the training needs of practicing teachers within their regions, as well as to reduce the gap between what is known by researchers and innovators and what is practiced by teachers throughout the nation.

References

Bruner, J.S. _Toward a Theory of Instruction._ New York: W.W. Norton and Co., 1966.
Hall, R.V., Panyan, M., Rabon, D. and Broden, M. Instructing Beginning Teachers in Reinforcement Procedures Which Improve Classroom Control. _Journal of Applied Behavior Analysis,_ 1968, 1, 315-322.
Mager, R.F. _Preparing Instructional Objectives._ Palo Alto: Fearon Publishers, 1962.
McLarey, C. and Bonk, E.C. Test Interpretation Kit I. Garland, Texas: Carmen Productions, 1968.
Popham, W.J. and Baker, E. Filmstrip-Tape Programs. Los Angeles: Vimcet Associates, 1969.
Skinner, B.F. _The Technology of Teaching._ New York: Appleton-Century-Crofts, 1968.

Dale D. Baum and **Thomas G. Chastain** are with the Special Education Instructional Materials Center, University of Kansas, Lawrence.

TULSAPAC: Anatomy of a Learning Package

Bruce Howell

Within a large city school system, an observer would typically be able to record a microcosm of perceptions and stages of learning package developments. He might observe an individual teacher quite capably incorporating the concept, but would draw a vacant stare from another when he requests comparative information. Moving on, he might note the "read about it, then implement it" prescription espoused by some administrators. Later, reflecting on his research, the observer might conclude that, in this one school system, he has reviewed examples of the chronological spectrum of progress in the development and utilization of learning packages. It is this phenomenon—the variation in levels of understanding—that prompted development of a program designed to promote equality of perception and a basis for standardization of a learning package format in the Tulsa, Oklahoma, school system.

Tulsa, a city that includes 78,000 school-age children, employs a staff of 3,500 teachers. One hundred and ten school buildings, including eighty elementary, twenty junior high and ten senior high schools, comprise the facilities. Varying student economic and ethnic factors can be noted within neighborhood attendance districts in this total school population. Student mobility ranges from 4 to 127 percent annually in different schools. Compounding this student mobility problem is a twenty percent annual turnover in teaching staff, that results in a constant cycle of teachers with varying experiences and backgrounds. One must only list variables such as these that contribute to general discontinuity to understand why progress in implementing a standard concept of the learning package has been considerably limited in large systems.

The learning package based on identified and measured behavioral change is, we believe, the best tool available for implementing techniques of individualizing instruction on a non-graded design. With some technical clarification it may become the educator's best answer to the challenges of account-ability. Recognizing this potential, some members of the super-visory staff of the Tulsa Public Schools have attempted to assimilate and interpret data that would provide a foundation for a standard concept and format for the learning package in the Tulsa school system. Two objectives have encompassed these efforts: (1) to identify and promote standardization of the learning package format and that of one of its basic components, the behavioral objective, and (2) to illustrate this standardization by publication of learning packages authored by various departmental supervisors. The latter objective has also provided opportunity for the supervisor to articulate his particular program within a standard framework.

Development of the TULSAPAC by supervisors is not mandatory. Three years have lapsed since distribution of the first package, and a few have not yet participated. Consequently, it is not difficult to "quality control" each one developed. As instigator of this project, the author has assumed the quality control task, and it has proven beneficial as a standardization mechanism. Supervisors also review each other's efforts prior to submitting a preliminary draft.

TULSAPAC Components

Since a basic component of the learning package is the behavioral objective, it was first necessary to establish a format for writing objectives. This was locally defined as the "givens," the "will be ables" and the "level of acceptable accuracy." Thus, the TULSAPAC author merely filled in his content, expectations and minimum of acceptable accuracy. Since the writing of behavioral objectives was a new experience for most supervisors, most behavioral objectives were in the cognitive domain. However, since the first TULSAPACS were designed to be self-pacing and self-inclusive, cognitive objectives were quite applicable. Prepared as a means for home study, it was necessary that procedures for evaluating behavioral progress, such as check lists and response-verification sheets, be utilized in the packages.

Besides providing a standard model, early TULSAPACS focused on apprising principals of developments in the curriculum areas they were administrating.

Each learning package includes four sections:
1. Curriculum objectives
2. The program content and sequence
3. Means of evaluating a classroom
4. Contemporary trends.

Each section is composed of three components: (1) the behavioral objective, (2) a list of activities designed to provide the background for behavioral change, and (3) a means of evaluating progress toward behavioral change. These components comprise Tulsa's concept of the learning package. In reality, the TULSA-PAC is a compound learning package, since the format of three components in each section was repeated for each of the four sections, with four objectives, four activities and four sets of specific evaluative materials. Learning packages for students and teachers have also followed the TULSAPAC format.

A limited amount of creative license is permitted each supervisor in addition to the basic components. Acknowledgments, preface statements, diagrams and supplemental Appendix materials can also be included. However, compact and concise TULSAPACS are encouraged, and those incorporating these characteristics have proven to be most popular with the consumer.

TULSAPAC Examples

Selected examples of several learning packages are included below. These examples are representative of the organization of a "typical" TULSAPAC. The following Table of Contents illustrates the organizational arrangement of a TULSAPAC written for Business Education.

The TULSAPAC user usually reviews the content of the packages on the basis of independent study, and completes each section as a self-paced activity. Therefore, test keys must be available for immediate verification. As TULSAPACS are revised, authors are encouraged to define some objectives affectively as well as cognitively.

Examples of behavioral objectives are listed below that represent the four sections of study in each TULSAPAC.

Regarding *curriculum objectives:*
Given a list of 28 goals for public school art, the participant will be able to select with 100 percent accuracy the seven goals identified by art educators as being most pertinent to learning.

Given 20 statements, the participant will be able to select with 100 percent accuracy, five statements that express the purposes and philosophy of Home and Family Life Education.

Given a list of 20 items, the participant will be able to select, with 100 percent accuracy, six characteristics which describe a good developmental reading program.

Regarding *program sequence:*
Given a list of 24 reading skills and six main headings, the participant will categorize, with 80 percent accuracy, the skills under the proper headings.

Given a list of 20 concepts taught in elementary mathematics, the participant will be able to check four, with 100 percent accuracy, in which the subject matter is spiraled throughout all six grades.

Given a chart of grade levels and a list of subdivisions and major content areas of science, the participant will be able to complete the chart, with 100 percent accuracy, by listing the subdivisions or content areas on the chart at the proper grade level.

Regarding *means of evaluating a classroom:*
Given ten learning goals from foreign language courses and four class activities related to each goal, the participant will be able to select, with 70 percent accuracy, the activity which represents the best student-teacher interaction for a given purpose.

Given a list of 20 activities, the participant will select, with 100 percent accuracy, the five most important activities which are conducive to a properly structured kindergarten environment.

Given information concerning the prescribed daily classroom organization and procedures, the participant will be able to identify the basic sequence for a daily program, with 100 percent accuracy.

Regarding *contemporary trends:*

> *Given a list of eight issues from the Vocational Amendments of 1968, the participant will be able to list, with 100 percent accuracy, those issues of the Act that should be implemented as innovative and exemplary.*

> *Given 12 trends in modern girls' physical education programs, the participant will be able to select three that are most relevant to Tulsa.*

> *Given a list of seven major approaches to learning and a list of basic reading programs which are available from the list of state adoptions plus those reading programs currently used in Tulsa which are not available on the state list, the participant will match, with 100 percent accuracy, the reading program with the learning approach it uses.*

Another organizational aspect of all TULSAPACs is the arrangement of package components within each of the four areas. Two examples are shown below. The first illustrates an activity that will broaden understanding of evaluating procedures in a foreign language classroom. It is a sample of self-pacing activities designed for section three of the standard TULSAPAC format, *means for evaluating a classroom.* In this instance the foreign language supervisor has stated the objective, prepared appropriate activities, and referred the participant to a page for evaluation.

SECTION III

EVALUATING A CLASSROOM FOR EFFECTIVE FOREIGN LANGUAGE TEACHING

Behavioral Objective: Given ten learning goals from foreign language courses and three class activities related to each, the participant will be able to select, with 70 percent accuracy, the activity which represents the best student-teacher interaction for a purpose given.

Activities: Watch video tape (seven minutes) of a first level French class, eighth grade from Horace Mann Junior High, Mrs. Esther Griffith, teacher. (The video tape is available in Instructional Media, room 615, Education Service Center, Tulsa Public Schools.) Check five points of an effective foreign language classroom observed in the video tape, using the check list below.

CHECK LIST
1. Teacher speaks foreign language.
2. Students have ample opportunity to speak foreign language in groups and alone.
3. Students speak foreign language as if it were more important to try out the sounds than to imitate perfectly, although standard speech is heard and imitated.
4. Students speak foreign language with natural gestures, body movement and expression, as if they know what they are saying.
5. Students speak foreign language readily.
6. Teacher gives students time enough to answer.
7. Students have a chance to succeed.
8. Classroom activities are scheduled so that the skills of listening, speaking, reading and writing can be practiced.
9. Classroom activities are diversified with the attention span of adolescents in mind.
10. Physical set-up of room permits students to practice speaking with each other part of the class period.
11. Teacher uses visual aids, inflection and gesture to make meaning clear, and translates as a last resort.
12. Translation is used in modern language classes as cautiously as red hot chilis.
13. Students listen to each other as well as to teacher and to tapes.

14. Teacher pinpoints objective of listening, reading or repeating.
15. Student is never interrupted, nor corrected while presenting a skit before the class.
16. Original composition, oral or written, is controlled (Quest).
17. Supplementary reading material on several levels is available.
18. Writing reinforces what has been learned orally.
19. Posters and other student work show that students relate the language, especially in Latin classes, to their own lives.
20. Learning another language looks like fun.

The second example, an exercise regarding *curriculum objectives,* has been prepared by the Supervisor of Economics Education in Tulsa. The sequential arrangement of the activities illustrates the process of leading the participant to conclusions regarding the objectives of economics. The video tape dialogue provides the participant with an alternative to the reading assignment. The "listing" activity provides a means for closure and is the exercise that promotes desired behavioral changes.

Following the procedural format, the Economics Supervisor then instructs the participant to evaluate his understanding by attempting the post-test.

SECTION I

Behavioral Objective: Given a list of twenty-four areas in Economics, the participant can select, with 100 percent accuracy, six areas which have been identified by educators and economists as necessary for competent decision-making by the citizens of the United States.

Activities: 1. Read: DEEP PART I. James Calderwood. Joint Council on Economic Education. Pp. ix, 1 and 2. As you read, list in writing the six areas in Economics identified as necessary for decision-making by citizens.

2. Video tape: (10 minutes) Professor Lorraine Scheer, economist (The University of Tulsa); Clayton Millington, educator (Oklahoma State University); Edith Todd, classroom teacher (Revere); Constance McAnnallen, classroom teacher (Skelly), on *The Major Areas in Economics Necessary for Decision-Making.*

3. List the areas in Economics which consultants believe to be necessary for competent decision-making.

When you have completed the activities you are ready for the Self-Test for SECTION I, page 19.

These examples illustrate the basic structural segments of the learning package, (1) the overall organization, (2) the model used to write the behavioral objective, and (3) the format selected for specific objectives and activities. To date, nineteen learning packages have been printed for in-service utilization, all of which follow the preceding design. Available TULSAPACs are:

Kindergarten Education
Social Studies in Elementary Schools
Reading, a Process
Mathematics for the Elementary School
Science Education
Art Education
The English Language Arts
Economic Education
Elementary Physical Education
Secondary Boys' Physical Education
Foreign Languages
Business Education
Vocational and Technical Education
Home and Family Life Education
Secondary Mathematics
Industrial Arts Education
The School Library
Writing and Implementing Behavioral Objectives

TULSAPAC Implementation

Dissemination has been focused on two groups of educators in the Tulsa system, the administrator and the teacher. However, interest has also developed among members of other departments in the Tulsa school system. For example, this interest has evolved into a TULSAPAC on Human Relations prepared by members of that department.

Introduction of the learning package concept to administrators was initially promoted as one phase of an Administrator Development Program designed to provide continuing education on *contemporary educational trends.* Consultants, simulated materials, instructional media and interaction sessions were utilized to provide principals with a common background on trends. Small study groups also emerged from the large-group sessions based on topics of mutual interest.

Two of the sessions focused directly on techniques for individualizing instruction. Information on this process was reviewed through large-group presentations. In order to enhance individual understanding of this process, the TULSAPACs were used. They provided principals with advance information on the learning package format proposed for use in Tulsa, a major factor in promoting standardization. Tulsa principals can now speak with some authority on the topic of learning packages and their components—they have used them.

Development and promotion of system-wide activities is a responsibility of the Division of Instruction in Tulsa. Supervisors are required to conduct appropriate sessions pertaining to contemporary trends in their respective fields. Consequently, the dissemination of a standard learning package format was not difficult the second year. Utilizing their respective TULSAPACs as an instructional device, supervisors were able to exemplify the process.

In addition to the departmental in-service meetings directed by supervisors, two general in-service classes were conducted, entitled "Writing and Implementing Behavioral Objectives." A special TULSAPAC bearing this title was written for these sessions.

Interest in this teaching technique can be measured not only by the large attendance at these sessions, but by noting several group efforts by teachers. Various departmental staffs in five junior high schools have cooperatively teamed together and designed models of continuous progress, using the learning package as the basic teaching tool. A group of upper grade elementary teachers have joined efforts and written a sequence of learning packages combining social studies and reading. Two elementary schools utilizing a continuous progress curriculum based on a continuum of learning packages recently opened. This will culminate three years of preparatory activities. A "little school" based on this new design and utilizing a sequence of learning packages has opened. Its companion "big school" will maintain the traditional program with a graded curriculum, thus affording parents in that particular neighborhood attendance area the option of selecting either design. Thus, the immediate impact of the TULSAPAC is tangibly evident in terms of teacher use. The intangibles regarding teachers' future attitudes and role perceptions concerning the development and utilization of learning packages remain to be determined.

Bruce Howell is Assistant Superintendent for Instruction, Tulsa (Oklahoma) Public Schools.

Program 100: Developing Instructional Systems to Improve Teaching Competencies

Charles C. Jung

The purpose of Program 100 is to develop instructional systems to improve teaching competencies in performing processes which complement the function of instruction. Such processes include (1) objective analysis and planning for classroom management, (2) interacting effectively in teamwork relationships, (3) supporting continued improvement of the school setting, (4) providing students with competencies as active learners and (5) interacting with students to develop planfulness in their use of thought processes so that personal meanings are derived from learning.

This article will argue that the procedures in our schools must change if we are to maintain the purpose of public education in America. The nature of current social change and the evolution of social-psychological self of today's youth are pressing for a fundamental educational reformation. The objectives of Program 100 will be presented as a response to this need. The strategy, development procedures and current progress in developing the instructional systems of Program 100 will be briefly reported.

Changing Procedures to Maintain the Purpose of Public Education

The purpose of public education is to maintain its society. In the past, society has been relatively static. Roles, organizations, community and societal configurations remained seemingly fixed for decades at a time. The schools needed to prepare individuals to fill these roles and maintain these constant relationships.

In the 20th century, and especially during the past 20 years, our society has experienced increasing rates of change.[1] To maintain such a society, our schools can no longer teach students to move into fixed roles, organizations or communities. To maintain society in a world of change, the schools must prepare students to expect, and cope with, real-world phenomena in more dynamic terms. Instead of learning a role, students need to learn what roles are and how to move in and out of them. Instead of learning fixed bodies of knowledge, students must learn that knowledge will continue to change, and that it must be acquired continuously in relation to current issues. Students need to learn how to be learners—how to create conditions for their own continued learning. Instead of a fixed set of relationships, they need to learn how to move in and out of relationships without losing the human meanings of relating.

There was a time when the processes of being a formal learner did not need to be maintained by most members of our society. It was only important that they retain as much of the content of what they had learned during their school years as possible. Now the situation is reversed. Much content that is learned will become antiquated and should be forgotten or replaced. The processes of being a learner must be retained.

At the Northwest Regional Educational Laboratory, we believe that the very nature of current social change has altered. Cultural and technological evolution have advanced to a point where man has achieved ultimate kinds of creative and destructive capability. Our philosophical understandings of what it means to be alive are being called into question.[2] Our schools must aid the transition from a static to a dynamic orientation.

Put simply, our citizens need to gain personally useable understandings of processes. These include intrapersonal processes of understanding and developing one's self. They include interpersonal processes of relating to and working with others. They include the processes of being a learner. They include the processes of working in, and operating, organizations which can be dynamic in new kinds of objectives and utilizing new kinds of resources. We believe it is valid to claim that process has become our most important product.[3]

An obvious implication is that educators must have expertise in the processes of dynamic functioning if they are to help students gain such processes. Schools need to move to new kinds of objectives (e.g., employability of all high school graduates, or the competencies of self-directed learning) and utilize new kinds of resources (modular scheduling, team teaching). Such changes call for expertise in the processes of analyzing, planning and personal and organizational teamwork. With increasing frequency, they call for expertise in processes of relating to, and working with, the community which the school serves.

We believe there are less obvious, and more critical, reasons why improved competencies in processes are needed. We believe that increasing numbers of today's youth are fundamentally different from most citizens of past societies. In most societies of the past, most citizens had stereotypic understandings of who they were. In societies which supported individualism, citizens could evolve to a kind of opinionated social-psychological understanding of their selves. The technology of our current society presents individuals with relativistic, cross-cultural awarenesses. Many of our youth are evolving to an existential kind of self-awareness which is both dangerous and exciting in its implications for society. The danger lies in the temporary rejection of traditional normative behaviors which can accompany the existential self orientation. The excitement lies in the increased range of human potential which can be achieved by the individual who continues to evolve, beyond the existential self, to a creative self orientation.[4] It appears that we are living in a millennium period of human transition. A new level of social-psychological self-evolution is possible. It is necessary if we are to avoid polarized conflicts and self-destruction. On this basis, we advance a more fundamental argument for the need of mastering process competencies in our public schools. Personally useable understanding of such processes is the basis for evolving to the kind of self from which an individual accepts responsibility for who and what he is and his contribution to the world of which he is a part. The less obvious, critical implication for education is that certain intra-personal and interpersonal processes must be employed in operating schools, and included within the curriculum, to facilitate the evolution of individuals toward a creative social-psychological self.

In summary, immediate priorities for educational reformation in this country include the following:

1. Learners need to be prepared for a world of change. They need to exit the formal educational system with the orientation and skills of continuous learners.

2. The operation of schools needs to shift in emphasis from static to dynamic capabilities. Educators need competencies of using processes to repeatedly change the kinds of objectives they are working toward and the kinds of resources they are employing to achieve them.

3. Educators, and the public to whom they are responsible, need increased sophistication in analyzing the learner and society as the referents for assessing educational effectiveness. If our emerging models of societal change and social-psychological self evolution are valid, then current emphasis on evaluating schools in terms of what the learner has learned will need to be complemented with techniques for assessing what the learner is becoming in terms of self evolution.

4. Individualizing instruction in terms of readiness is finally beginning to be attended to by educators. It must be complemented by individualizing in terms of relevance. Relevance is defined as influence on the social-psychological self. Conditions for learning will vary dramatically, dependent on the phase of an individual's self evolution. The formulas for learning processes which apply to lower forms of animals have decreasing applicability to human beings as they evolve a complete social-psychological self. Multimillion-dollar curriculum reform efforts, constructed with brilliant attention to the structure of the content and concern for reinforcement, have failed to engage learners. Greater attention must be given to the issue of relevance.

The Objectives of Program 100

There are two kinds of rationale for "Program 100: Developing Instructional Systems to Improve Teacher Competencies." The first is that competencies in using the processes for which these instructional systems train increase the pragmatic effectiveness of educators. Teachers interact with students in such a way that more learning takes place. Also, the learning that takes place is more relevant to the students. Teachers identify problems more objectively and work for improvements more rationally. Educators are more open to innovations and more efficient in working together. Students understand and accept their role as learners more actively.

The second kind of rationale goes beyond the desirability of improving ongoing practices by better use of processes. Personally useable understandings of the processes provided by Program 100 instructional systems represent a dynamic, rather than static, orientation. Instead of waiting for a set of materials to provide an area of curriculum, you gain competencies to retrieve, adapt or create the needed area of curriculum. Instead of always attempting to influence students to take in certain knowledge and respond with certain behaviors, you use your own teaching behaviors in response to meanings being exhibited by learners. Instead of only being reactive to problematic conditions and striving for symptoms of success, you repeatedly diagnose and assess how and why things are happening as they are. The role of educators becomes one of managing resources to provide functions which facilitate learning, rather than one of repeating a routine set of tasks. In this dynamic orientation, the learner becomes active in providing these tasks and functions for himself. This facilitates self evolution of the learner.

Today's educators need competencies in processes which guarantee learner outcomes while also guaranteeing evolution of the self of each individual learner. These include six categories of processes which (1) facilitate students in becoming active, independent learners; (2) provide pupil-teacher interaction responsive to the pupil's involvement in deriving personal meaning for what he is learning; (3) concern each kind of criterion for objective analysis and planned change; (4) involve the basic skills of interpersonal effectiveness; (5) provide continued support for professional growth and organizational self renewal; and (6) apply process resources in a manner most appropriate to the local setting. Figure 1 indicates the instructional systems developed, or being developed, under each of these six categories.

Objectives of Program 100 are to develop the instructional systems which virtually guarantee trainee achievement of competencies in using the processes focused upon. A process is defined as a particular sequence of behaviors which provides a function. For example, Corrigan's version of system technology[5] is a logical, analytical "process" which can be used for the functions of planning or managing. Specific objectives for each competency are stated as part of the instructional system. For example, here is the objective for Subset VII of the Research Utilizing Problem-Solving instructional system. "Given the force field analysis produced by Mrs. Jones and a total of nine data gathering tools in Chapter 2, 3 and 4 of the SRA booklet, 'Diagnosing Classroom Learning Environments,' and given the principles in the SRA booklet for determining appropriate tools for data collection, participants will be able to select six tools relevant to data gathering requirements specific to Mrs. Jones' force field analysis."

The instructional systems in the category Teaching for Affective Growth deal with competencies of learning to learn and the evolution of a creative, responsible self. Self-Directed Mini-Packages, for example, focus on such topics as "Getting and Using Help," "Letting Yourself Be Influenced," "Checking for Understanding" and "Coping with Feeling Dumb."

Instructional systems in the category Pupil-Teacher Interaction give teachers competencies in using behaviors responsive to pupils' efforts to make meaning out of what they are learning. Pupils of such teachers would ultimately be capable of making such determinations as "I need more data to clarify that concept," or "I'm generalizing when I should be testing a hypothesis."

The Objective Analysis and Planned Change category is concerned with competencies for appropriate use of problem-solving processes for improvements which are based on technical

Figure 1

Six Categories of Instructional Systems in Program 100

Teaching For Affective Growth	Pupil-Teacher Interaction	Objective Analysis and Planned Change	Interpersonal Relations	Preparing Education Training Consultants	Education As a System To Promote Human Potential
*Cross-Age Peer Help	*Systematic and Objective Analysis of Instruction	*Research Utilizing Problem-Solving	*Interpersonal Communications	†Skills Training	Schools to Support Growth
†300 Self-Directed Mini-Packages	*Interaction Analysis	†System Technology	†Interpersonal Conflict	†Consultation	
Providing For Affective Growth	*Higher Level Thought Processes	Understanding Conflict and Negotiations	Interpersonal Decision-Making	†Organizational Development	
Aesthetic Aspects of Learning	*Inquiry	Needs Assessment	Professional Self-Renewal	Organizational Self-Renewal	
	†Teaching Responsively to Individualize Meaning	Creative Problem-Solving			

*These seven instructional systems have been completed.
†These instructional systems are under development.

criteria, theoretical criteria or philosophical criteria. It assumes educators need to be able to be accountable for achieving objectives they say they are responsible for, for knowing how and why things are occurring as they are in the school setting, and for negotiating with various interest groups concerning the legitimate range of objectives for which the schools should provide. Instructional systems in the Interpersonal Relations category provide competencies basic to efficient teamwork in any productive enterprise. As the teacher isolation of the self-contained classroom gives way to team efforts, these interpersonal behaviors need to be assured.

The instructional systems in the category Preparing Education Training Consultants provide competencies to support continuous professional growth of educators. It is anticipated that approximately one out of every hundred educators needs such competencies to support self-renewal of individuals, and of school systems as organizations, in a society of continuous evolutionary change.

The instructional system in the category Education As a System To Support Human Potential is for use in school systems whose personnel have mastered competencies of most of the other systems. It is for managing the allocation of process resources of the system in a manner most appropriate to local requirements and constraints.

The Strategy of Program 100

The major requirement of Program 100 instructional systems is that they provide all trainees, who enter the system under appropriate designated conditions, with basic competencies to perform the process being trained for. The emphasis is on "do it" capability in addition to objectives which are simply "know it."

An additional requirement is that the instructional systems must be mass diffusible. This has meant that such systems must be low-cost, replicable by non-expert trainers, and acceptable to higher education institutions for course credit-granting status.

Need for low cost has constrained Program 100 from using such technology as audio-visual behavioral feedback or extensive instructional films. Cassette tape recorders and inter-trainee observations are used for behavioral feedback. Expertise and assessment techniques are built into the materials rather than relying on the person conducting the training to provide them. The function of instruction is provided by the trainees for themselves and each other by virtue of the materials and kinds of activities they are directed to perform.

This has made the training replicable by trainers who are not expert in the processes being trained for. The trainer need only be familiar with the role of conducting the training, which generally is provided by his having had one experience with the system in the role of a trainee. The quality of trainee reactions and outcomes has led to the majority of teacher training institutions in the northwest states to use these instructional systems for course credit.

A Program 100 instructional system typically includes the following materials. A leader's manual gives instructions for each step of the design, approximate time needed, objectives of each subunit, materials and preparation necessary and the rationale of each step of the design. Brief motion pictures or overhead projectuals are sometimes included. Consumable participant materials include instructions for learning activities, theory inputs, observation guides, stimulation information and assessment techniques. Training is generally conducted in a workshop setting, with from eighteen to thirty-six participants over a period of from two to eight days. Some systems include work done on an individual basis, including practice in one's own classroom between workshop sessions. An important trade-off should be noted in evaluating the kind of training provided by these instructional systems. They virtually guarantee achievement of basic "know it" and "do it" competencies for any trainee who goes through the system as designed. They do not guarantee the relevance of these outcomes, or the forms of training experiences provided, to all individuals.

It is critical that participants enter the training with valid expectations and a desire for appropriate outcomes. There is no allowance for the trainee to digress from the prestructured design into areas of personal interest which might be identified. Such digression is explicitly ruled out under the assumption that most persons who will be conducting the training do not have trainer competencies to help individuals with personal growth in process areas.[6] Individuals who desire such "sensitivity training"-type learning experiences should seek them from appropriate professionals.[7] Sensitivity training, appropriately conducted, can maximize relevance of process kinds of growth, but cannot guarantee any specific outcomes. Program 100 instructional systems provide basic competencies for conducting specific processes, but are only appropriate to those who have identified their relevance.

The issue of individualizing instruction poses some problems in Program 100 instructional systems. Much of this training is interpersonal in nature and can't be learned effectively alone. This, and the cost advantage of having behavioral feedback provided by other trainees, results in designs in which several individuals are paced together through the macrostructure of the training design. This results in some complaints of going "too fast" or "too slow." This is counteracted by including material which allows individuals to go broader or deeper at times than the minimal outcomes which the designers saw as necessary to performing the process in question.

It should also be noted that most of this training is not prescriptive in nature. It does not have the effect of saying, "You should always teach like this!" Rather, each instructional system focuses on a process that most teachers will sometime feel the need of using. The training puts the competencies of performing that process in the teacher's repertoire. The teacher will then be able to prescribe its use when desired. The systems sometimes suggest a rationale for when and why the teacher would use the process in relation to learner needs and the particular, individual style of the teacher. But, it is always up to the teacher to decide in any particular instance.

Development Procedures in Program 100

Program 100 follows a sequence of 37 events used by the Northwest Regional Educational Laboratory in developing products. These are included in five stages, labeled: Concept Stage, Feasibility Stage, Operational Planning Stage, Development Stage and Installation Stage.

These phases progress through four kinds of evaluation as an instructional system is developed. While working on the prototype of the system, concern is primarily for the feasibility of providing the necessary low-cost type of training for the process in question in a manner acceptable to teachers. While working on the interim form of the system, concern is for arriving at a design that guarantees trainee performance of outcome objectives. There is simultaneous work on creating materials and valid, reliable assessment techniques. In completing the system as a training resource, a field test is conducted to determine conditions related to outcomes and applications of the training. Longitudinal, operational testing is planned for the final years of the program to determine the effects of application on learners.

It is expected the school systems applying the process competencies provided by Program 100 instructional systems will be dynamic and self-renewing in nature. Students coming from such systems will be significantly more active as continuous learners and will have evolved further along the dimension toward a creative, responsible self than students from the average school system of today. They not only will have learned well, they will be learners! They will be more capable people than today's average citizen, not just because of what they know, but because of the kind of people they are in terms of their social-psychological self-concept.

When extensive analysis is needed while working on a system, Corrigan's version of system technology[8] has been applied (see Figure 2). A flow chart (see Figure 3) has been developed of events typically followed in the work of developing an instructional system. Cost estimates are derived from the systems charts, in a PPBS-type accounting and management process.

The Northwest Regional Educational Laboratory includes a Dissemination Division that relates to the Program 100 development staff in carrying out the final phases of making a product available in the field. Long before these final phases, the

Program 100 Analysis*

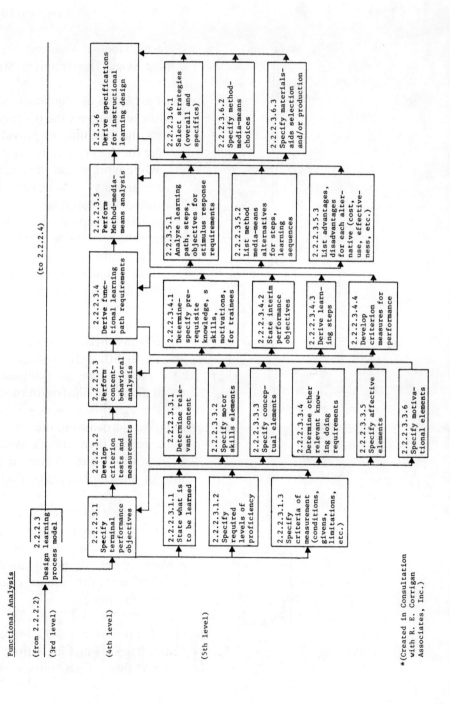

Functional Analysis

(from 2.2.2.2)

(3rd level)

2.2.2.3 Design learning process model

(to 2.2.2.4)

(4th level)

2.2.2.3.1 Specify terminal performance objectives

2.2.2.3.2 Develop criterion tests and measurements

2.2.2.3.3 Perform content-behavioral analysis

2.2.2.3.4 Derive functional learning path requirements

2.2.2.3.5 Perform Method-media-means analysis

2.2.2.3.6 Derive specifications for instructional learning design

(5th level)

2.2.2.3.1.1 State what is to be learned

2.2.2.3.1.2 Specify required levels of proficiency

2.2.2.3.1.3 Specify criteria of measurement (conditions, givens, limitations, etc.)

2.2.2.3.3.1 Determine relevant content

2.2.2.3.3.2 Specify motor skills elements

2.2.2.3.3.3 Specify conceptual elements

2.2.2.3.3.4 Determine other relevant knowing doing requirements

2.2.2.3.3.5 Specify affective elements

2.2.2.3.3.6 Specify motivational elements

2.2.2.3.4.1 Determine-specify prerequisite knowledge, skills, motivations for trainees

2.2.2.3.4.2 State interim performance objectives

2.2.2.3.4.3 Derive learning steps

2.2.2.3.4.4 Develop criterion measures for performance

2.2.3.5.1 Analyze learning path, steps, objectives for stimulus response requirements

2.2.3.5.2 List method media-means alternatives for steps, learning sequences

2.2.3.5.3 List advantages, disadvantages for each alternative (cost, use, effectiveness, etc.)

2.2.3.6.1 Select strategies (overall and specifics)

2.2.3.6.2 Specify method-media-means choices

2.2.3.6.3 Specify materials-aids selection and/or production

*(Created in Consultation with R. E. Corrigan Associates, Inc.)

Figure 3

Instructional System Development Flow Chart
(Continued on Pages 149, 150, 151)

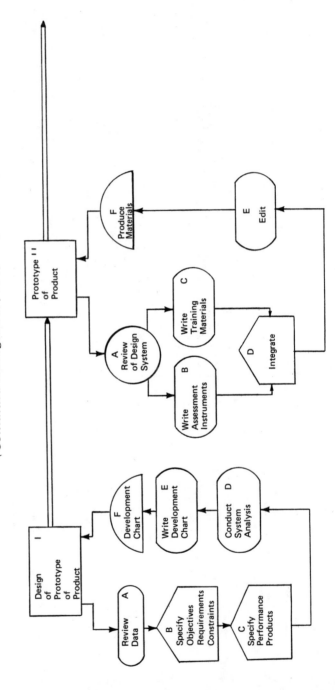

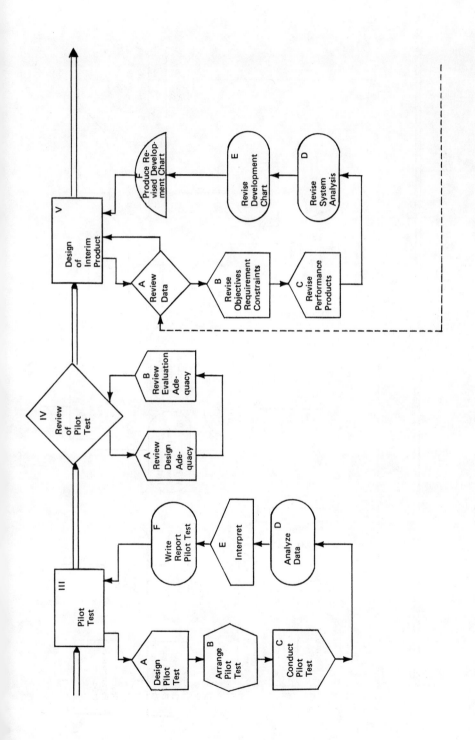

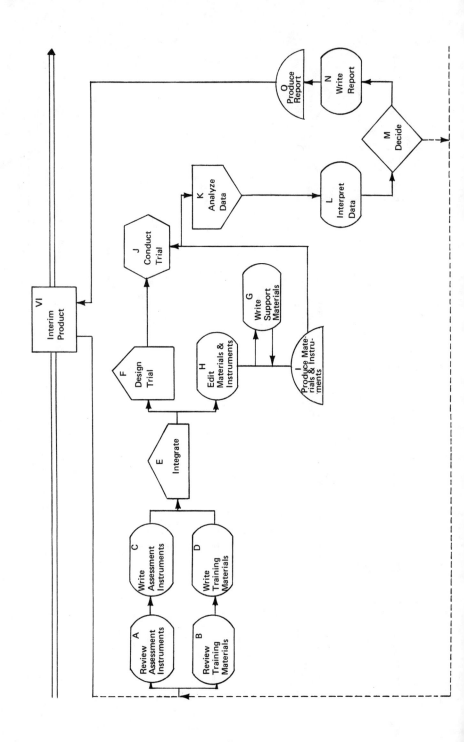

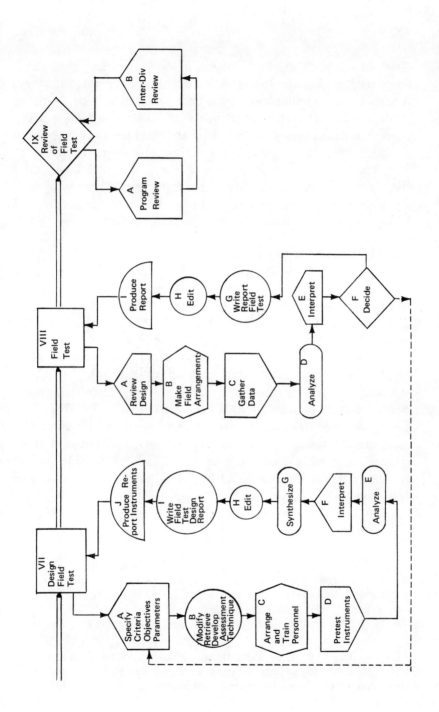

development staff will have worked in the field in a manner which supports the ultimate dissemination and implementation strategy. A high degree of collaboration has been achieved with personnel in school districts, state departments of education and teacher training institutions. Most field trial and field test costs have been provided by locally sponsored training workshops. From 50 to 120 trainers from among persons in key educational roles throughout the Northwest have been trained, mostly at local cost, for each instructional system. This process is now being replicated by regional representatives in other parts of the country.

Current Progress of Program 100

Seven of the twenty-three planned instructional systems have been completed. With adequate funding, the program can be finished in nine more years. The quality of the products and cost effectiveness of development procedures has increased steadily during the past five years. Training outcomes which cost $150 per trainee to achieve four years ago are now being achieved more rapidly, with greater trainee satisfaction and more objective assessment, for less than one-fifth the cost. There is explicit documentation of over 29,000 of the Northwest's 77,000 teachers having received training in one or another of the Program 100 instructional systems currently available. One or more of these systems are being used in over twenty states outside of the Northwest.* Versions have also been used in at least three foreign countries.

Notes

1. A. Toffler. *Future Shock*. New York: Random House, 1970.
2. C. Jung. The Nature and Problems of Change, chapter in a publication of the Improving State Leadership in Education Project, Denver, Colorado, 1971.
3. L. Rhodes. Linkage Strategies for Change: Process May Be the Product.

*The Northwest Regional Educational Laboratory serves Alaska, Hawaii, Idaho, Montana, Oregon and Washington. It has also worked extensively in Guam and the U.S. Trust Territories of the Pacific.

Phi Delta Kappan, Volume LI, No. 4, December, 1969.
4. C. Jung. *The Next Revolution: Education and the Evolution of Self.* Working paper, Northwest Regional Educational Laboratory, August, 1971.
5. R.E. Corrigan. *A System Approach for Education.* R.E. Corrigan Associates, Anaheim, California, 1969.
6. C. Jung. A Model of Developing Process Trainers. Position paper prepared for the National Training Laboratories, Institute for Applied Behavioral Science, September, 1969.
7. L. Bradford, J. Gibb and K. Benne (Editors). *T-Group Theory and Laboratory Method.* New York: John Wiley and Sons, 1964.
8. R.E. Corrigan. *SAFE Self Directed Training Series for Instructional Systems Designers.* R.E. Corrigan Associates, Anaheim, California, 1970.

Charles C. Jung is Coordinator of Program 100, Northwest Regional Educational Laboratory, Portland, Oregon.

Minicourses: Individualized Learning Packages for Teacher Education

Walter R. Borg

During the past four and one-half years, the major thrust of the Teacher Education Program at the Far West Laboratory for Educational Research and Development has been the development of Minicourses. Minicourses are individualized multi-media learning packages designed to help teachers develop instructional skills.

These skills are highly specific and within a given Minicourse relate to a single instructional strategy. For example, Minicourse No. 2 is designed to train the teacher in the use of fourteen skills that are useful in helping primary grade children develop better use of language (see Table 1). The format of the Minicourse is essentially different from that found in most conventional instruction. In taking the Minicourse, the trainee (usually an in-service teacher) spends about fifteen hours over a five-week period. These fifteen hours very strongly emphasize practice of the specific skills and feedback on the teacher's performance. In fact, only about ten percent of the teacher's time is devoted to being told about the skills through instructional films. About twenty percent of the teacher's time involves seeing examples of the skill as illustrated on the classroom clips and model films, while seventy percent of the teacher's time is devoted to practicing the skill and evaluating video- or audiotape recordings of his own teaching performance in order to obtain corrective feedback.

The components of a Minicourse package typically include the following:

a.   A *Teacher's Handbook* that provides the trainee with

information on the skills to be learned, written exercises and simulations to give the trainee initial practice, and forms used by the trainee in evaluating the videotape recordings of his teaching performance.

b. *Instructional films* which give the trainee a precise definition of each skill and show him short classroom clips in which the skills are used.

c. *Model films* which show the trainee how the skills can be applied in a regular lesson and require the trainee to recognize and discriminate among the various skills.

f. A *Coordinator's Handbook* that provides the course coordinator with information needed to set up and conduct the Minicourse in an in-service setting.

Table 1*

Minicourse 2 Objectives and Skills

INSTRUCTIONAL SEQUENCE 1

Objective   To develop skills useful for extending the language and thought of kindergarten children.

Covered Skills   Extending a phrase to a sentence.
Refining meaning by providing the pupil with a word that accurately describes the object or situation.

INSTRUCTIONAL SEQUENCE 2

Objective   To develop skills that introduce and provide practice in the use of new language patterns.

Covered Skills   Modeling a language pattern in context and, if possible, in conjunction with specific objects.
Eliciting language patterns from pupils.
Praising in specific terms, omitting the personal element.

*Reprinted from Borg, W.R., M.L. Kelley, P. Langer and M.D. Gall. The Minicourse—A Microteaching Approach to Teacher Education by permission of Macmillan Educational Services.

INSTRUCTIONAL SEQUENCE 3

Objective — To develop skills that facilitate pupil learning and use of positional words.

Covered Skills — Introducing specific positional words in context and in conjunction with concrete objects.
Providing varied physical experiences to assure pupil comprehension of positional words.
Eliciting pupil use of positional words.

INSTRUCTIONAL SEQUENCE 4

Objective — To develop skills that increase pupil ability to observe, describe and classify objects.

Covered Skills — Eliciting observations of objects.
Eliciting observations of similarities and differences among and within groups.
Providing language patterns for expressing comparisons.

INSTRUCTIONAL SEQUENCE 5

Objective — To develop skills that increase pupil ability to identify and describe action.

Covered Skills — Describing an action in conjunction with demonstrating it.
Introducing other actions that illustrate the verb.
Eliciting pupil use of the modeled verbs.

Table 2

Minicourse Development Schedule

		Scheduled Completion Date
Minicourse 1:	Effective Questioning in a Classroom Discussion (Elementary) has been commercially produced.	Complete, operational form now available
	Course Goal: To improve teacher skills related to questioning and conducting class discussions.	

Minicourse 2: Developing Children's Oral Language   Complete
operational form
now available

Course Goal: To increase teacher skills that encourage the acquisition of language.

Minicourse 3: Effective Questioning in a Classroom Discussion (Secondary)   Complete

Course Goal: To increase the effectiveness of the questioning techniques of secondary school teachers and the quantity and quality of student participation (grades 7-12) in class discussion situations.

Minicourse 4: Verbal Interaction   Complete

Course Goal: To train teachers to categorize their classroom behavior in the Flanders system.

Minicourse 5: Individualizing Instruction in Mathematics (Elementary)   Complete
operational form
now available

Course Goal: To increase teachers' effectiveness in diagnosis, demonstration of problem-solving procedures and evaluation of learning during math tutoring sessions; to increase the amount of time teachers spend in structured tutoring of students' math difficulties.

Minicourse 8* Organizing Independent Learning: Primary Level   Complete
operational form
now available

Course Goal: To provide primary teachers with a set of skills (organized procedures) that will make it

*Work on Minicourses 6 and 7 was halted after preliminary development.

possible for them to instruct, unin-
terrupted, a group of five children
for ten minutes, while the remaining twenty or more children work
independently.

Minicourse 9:	Higher Cognitive Questioning	Complete operational form now available
	Course Goal: To increase teacher effectiveness (grades 4-8) in asking questions which require the use of complex thinking skills.	
Minicourse 10:	Role Playing as an Instructional Technique	Complete
	Course Goal: To train teachers in the use of role-playing skills for wide-range application in the class-room.	
Minicourse 11:	Teaching Skills that Develop Inde-pendent Learning in the Secondary Classroom.	December, 1972
	Course Goal: To develop teacher skills that facilitate learner indepen-dence in a wide range of subject areas.	
Minicourse 12:	Interaction Analysis as a Guide to Classroom Change	May, 1973
	Course Goal: To train teachers to be able to make systematic changes in their classrooms based on inter-action analysis data.	
Minicourse 13:	Expository Teaching	November, 1972
	Course Goal: To increase secondary teacher effectiveness in explaining and in conveying information through the use of oral exposition.	

Minicourse 14: A Discussion Approach to Contro-   Complete
                versial Issues

                Course 'Goal: To develop teacher
                and pupil skills in discussion and
                critical appraisal of controversial
                social issues.

Minicourse 15: Teaching Skills that Develop Inde-   Complete
                pendent Learning in the Upper Ele-
                mentary Years.

                Course Goal: To develop teacher
                skills that facilitate learner indepen-
                dence in a wide range of subject
                areas.

Minicourse 16: Peer and Cross-Age Tutoring   December, 1972

                Course Goal: To train pupils in
                skills needed to function effectively
                as tutors of their peers or younger
                pupils.

Minicourse 17: The Use of Role-Playing in the   June, 1973
                Social Sciences

                Course Goal: To develop teacher
                skills in using role-playing tech-
                niques to demonstrate and analyze
                social and governmental situations.

Minicourse 18: Teaching to Increase Reading Profi- Complete
                ciency

                Course Goal: To develop teacher
                skill in the use of instructional
                procedures that improve student
                learning in the area of reading.

Minicourse 19: Inquiry Strategies to be Used in the May, 1973
                Classroom

                Course Goal: To develop teacher

skill in the use of multiple inquiry
strategies in the elementary classroom.

Minicourse 20:   Divergent Thinking   Complete

Course Goal: To help the teacher to
establish a classroom environment
and to use teaching techniques that
encourage divergent thinking.

Minicourse 21:   Problem-Solving   Complete

Course Goal: To help the teachers
in the intermediate grades to set up
problem-solving situations, and assist students in developing problem-
solving tactics.

Minicourse 22:   Teaching Reading Comprehension   Complete

Course Goal: To develop teacher
skill in the use of instructional
procedures that improve student
reading comprehension.

Current Status of the Minicourse Program

At present five packages, Minicourses 1, 2, 5, 8 and 9, are
available on the commercial market for operational use. Twelve
additional Minicourses are at various points in the research and
development cycle.* Many of these courses are available from the
Far West Laboratory for experimental use only. It is anticipated
that three or four Minicourses will be released to the commercial
publisher each year.

Developing Program Objectives

An early task of the Laboratory was to make an assessment

*See Table 2 for title, course goal and estimated completion date of each
Minicourse.

of educational needs. This assessment, in turn, was to be used to identify areas in which the Laboratory should launch R & D programs. One of the areas identified as being strongly in need of improvement was teacher education.

Our next step was to review the professional and research literature in teacher education to determine whether available evidence supported the outcome of the needs survey. This review indicated that teacher education was indeed an area much in need of improvement. Since the Laboratory's resources were limited, the entire area of teacher education was too broad to constitute a viable R & D target. Thus, our next task was to identify the specific outcomes in teacher education that we would seek to achieve.

Teacher education programs are usually divided into three major areas. The first area, and the one in which pre-service programs have typically been most effective, is providing the teacher with the basic content that he is to teach. The second major area of teacher education is frequently labeled "professional foundations" and is concerned primarily with providing the teacher with a foundation of knowledge from the behavioral sciences and the education profession. Much of this knowledge is aimed at improving the teacher's understanding of the learner and the learning process, such as courses in human development, human learning and educational psychology. Other courses are designed to initiate the teacher as a member of the profession and provide him with certain essential skills, such as educational evaluation.

The third major area of teacher education is concerned with teaching methods. It is taught through a combination of courses in general and special methods plus student teaching. The real concern of these courses is to help teachers and potential teachers develop the basic skills of teaching. However, methods courses have been broadly condemned as of little value in helping the trainee develop specific teaching skills. When one looks at the typical methods course, it is apparent that most such courses are still attempting to develop skills by giving the trainee lectures on how to teach. There is no reason to expect this approach to be effective, since it is extremely difficult to learn any skill merely by being told how to do it.

Student teaching, on the other hand, is generally regarded as the most effective aspect of current teacher preparation programs. Recent evidence, however, casts serious doubt on the effectiveness of conventional student teaching approaches. Research by Joyce (1969), for example, shows that during the process of student teaching, the trainees in his sample became more directive and more punitive. A recent study at the University of Florida has also shown that the classroom performance of trainees in a conventional student teaching program can change for the worse. In this study, each trainee conducted a discussion lesson during the first week of student teaching and another, comparable lesson approximately five weeks later. Both lessons were recorded on videotape and transcripts of the lessons were analyzed to measure several specific performance variables related to class discussion. Trainees asked more fact questions and fewer higher-order questions, answered their own questions more frequently, asked more questions that would be answered with a single word, and talked more after five weeks of student teaching. In fact, for the ten discussion skills measured, trainee performance became poorer on nine after student teaching experience (Shea and Mould, 1971).

A look at the overall condition of teacher education led us to conclude that the most critical need for improvement was in the basic teaching skills area. Thus, the initial direction of our program moved towards identifying and specifically defining basic teaching skills and then developing educational experiences that would bring about substantial improvement in the teacher's use of the skills identified. As now defined, the broad goal of the Teacher Education Program is to develop a system for training teachers in basic teaching skills. The Minicourse packages will make up a substantial part of that system, but the program will also contain training packages built upon other instructional models. When complete, the system will provide the trainee with a repertoire of basic teaching skills related to a variety of instructional strategies. The system will also contain materials designed to help the trainee select the appropriate skills from his repertoire when confronted with a specific instructional problem.

Each Minicourse has specific performance objectives that are defined early in the R & D sequence and used subsequently to evaluate the package. These objectives are usually stated in terms of desired changes in the classroom performance of the trainee. However, whenever it is possible to establish a direct linkage between the performance of the trainee and the achievement and/or behavior of his pupils, we also evaluate pupil performance. For example, in Minicourse 8, teachers were trained to elicit problem solutions from pupils. Teacher mastery of this skill was evaluated in part by measuring the number of times pupils gave problem solutions in pre- and post-course classroom recordings (Borg, Kelley, Langer and Gall, 1970). Changes in pupil performance, of course, must be the ultimate criterion for measuring the effectiveness of any program concerned with teacher education.

The Minicourse Instructional Model

Having identified the program goals, our next task was to decide what kinds of educational experiences should be provided to bring about the desired outcomes and to combine these experiences into an instructional model. Much of our initial work in the development of the Minicourse instructional model was built directly upon the research on microteaching that had been conducted at Stanford University (Acheson, 1964; Allen and Fortune, 1966; Allen, Berliner, McDonald and Sobel, 1967; Allen and Ryan, 1969; and others).

However, we also looked at research and theoretical work in related areas, such as the studies on modeling carried out by Bandura and his associates (Bandura and Huston, 1961; Bandura and Kupers, 1963; Bandura, Ross and Ross, 1963; and others), research on effectiveness of media in teaching, such as the classic work of May and Lumsdaine (1958), and McDonald's work in skill training (1969). McDonald's work was especially useful in providing a theoretical base for the Minicourse model. He identified three elements that he considered essential in skills training. The first of these was a precise operational definition of the skill to be learned. The second was an opportunity to practice the skill, and the third was specific corrective feedback on the individual's performance of the skill. The microteaching research at Stanford had produced a prototype model that met McDonald's requirements.* Basic teaching skills had been identified and defined in operational terms. These were, for the most part, highly specific behavior patterns, such as use of prompting to elicit more complete pupil responses, redirection of the teacher's question to several pupils, and so on. The Stanford microteaching model used the microteach situation as a device for giving the learner an opportunity to practice the specific skills. Then, upon replaying a videotape recording of his microteach lesson, the learner received corrective feedback from a supervisor who focused very sharply on the skills being learned. Although the skill definitions and the amount of practice provided the learner both left something to be desired in the Stanford prototypes, the model did bring about statistically significant changes in the performance of the interns who participated. Thus, it appeared that if we could build educational experiences around an extension of the Stanford microteaching model, there would be a good chance that we could bring about substantial changes in the behavior of the trainee.

To illustrate the Minicourse instructional model and show how it meets McDonald's specifications, let us follow a trainee's experiences during a typical three-day instructional sequence taken from Minicourse 1, which deals with 12 specific skills that the elementary school teacher can apply to improve the use of questions in a discussion lesson.

On the first day of this sequence (Instructional Sequence 2), the trainee views an instructional film which defines three questioning skills: redirection, framing higher-order questions, and framing fact questions which require longer pupil responses. The instructional film also contains brief classroom sequences which

*Microteaching is a teaching situation in which the teacher teaches a short, simplified lesson (5-20 min.) to a small group of pupils, usually 4 to 10. It is based on the premise that the teacher can learn new skills more easily in the simple microteaching situation than in the more complex environment of the total classroom.

show teachers using these three skills. Immediately after the instructional film, the teacher-trainee views a model film which shows a model teacher incorporating all three skills into a brief lesson in which each technique is demonstrated several times. While he is viewing the film, the trainee's attention is focused on major points by visual cues and narrator comments, as these points are illustrated by the model teacher. A second version of the model film is then viewed. In this version, the skills are not identified and the trainee must recognize examples of each skill as they appear. The trainee also reads the appropriate chapter of the Teacher's Handbook, which supplements his information and tests his comprehension through a brief, self-administered quiz. He then prepares a ten-minute discussion lesson, again following handbook instructions. This lesson is based on his current class work, and is designed to provide practice in the three skills he has studied in the instructional and model films.

On the second day, the microteaching session is held.* The teacher conducts the lesson he has planned, using five or six of his own pupils. This presentation is recorded on videotape. The pupils then return to the regular classroom (manned in the meantime by a substitute, instructional aide or team teacher) and the teacher plays back the videotape. During the first playback, the teacher uses a self-evaluation form designed to help him appraise his overall performance on the three skills and identify the specific aspects of the lesson that might be improved. Viewing oneself on videotape often brings about an emotional reaction—the so-called cosmetic effect—which interferes with the teacher's objective evaluation of his performance. The first viewing gives the teacher a chance to get the cosmetic effect out of the way before doing a detailed analysis of his performance on the specific skills. The teacher again replays his lesson, this time using a checklist which emphasizes the skill of redirection. Based upon his evaluation of

---

*Teachers are usually given a free day for preparation between the instructional-model films and the microteaching session, and again between microteaching and reteaching. However, if time is limited, the course can be taken without scheduling any free days.

his performance, he replans his lesson so as to make better use of the three skills he is learning.

On the third day the teacher teaches his revised lesson (called the reteach lesson) using different pupils from his class, and the lesson again is recorded on videotape. The teacher then watches the playback of the lesson and evaluates his use of higher-order questions. He then replays his lesson again, this time evaluating his use of questions which call for longer pupil responses and analyzing the effect of such questions on his pupils. After school, two teachers who are taking the Minicourse view videotape replays of both of their reteach lessons for the third time, giving each other further feedback and suggestions for improving performance. An evaluation form is also provided for this third replay and, although this replay is optional, most teachers elect to do it.

You will note that the three days devoted to these skills provide a complete sequence of (1) instructional and model films, (2) microteaching with feedback and (3) reteaching with feedback, which constitutes the Minicourse instructional model. The typical Minicourse consists of three to six such sequences plus an introductory and practice lesson.

The instructional and model films give the trainee a very precise operational definition of each skill he is to learn, thus meeting McDonald's first requirement for effective skill training. The microteaching and reteach lessons permit the teacher to practice his skills under a simpler and less demanding situation than prevails in the full classroom, thus meeting the second requirement. The videotape replays provide specific feedback on the teaching performance of the trainee immediately after the lesson has been completed, thus meeting McDonald's third requirement.

How Minicourses Are Developed

Minicourses are developed by teams of professional educators and behavioral scientists on the Teacher Education Program staff. A typical team will consist of six persons: two Program Associates with doctoral-level training in education, psychology or a related behavioral science; two Program Assistants at the master's degree level who usually have some public school teaching experience; and two Research Clerks, who usually hold bachelor's degrees with training in education, a related behavioral science or in secretarial skills. A single team usually works on three Minicourses at a time, with each course being at a different stage in the R & D cycle.

The research and development cycle used in developing Minicourses consists basically of product development, field testing plus evaluation and revision. These steps are recycled until the Minicourse achieves the following two objectives:

1. The course brings about significant changes in the teaching performance of teachers participating in the field test.
2. The course is fully ready for operational use as an in-service training package in the public schools.

A Minicourse usually undergoes three field tests. However, if the objectives of any field test are not achieved, the test is repeated. The prototype Minicourse first undergoes a preliminary field test which is designed to provide formative evaluation data from a small sample of field test teachers. This test also permits an overall appraisal of course feasibility, and gives the team an opportunity to try out summative evaluation instruments that will be used in the next field test.

After revision, the main field test of the Minicourse is conducted. This field test emphasizes summative evaluation, i.e., determining whether teachers taking the course reach the criterion levels that have been established.

Again the course is revised as suggested by the field test results, and this revision undergoes an operational field test. The main purpose of this test is to determine whether school personnel can conduct the course in a satisfactory manner without any assistance from the Laboratory. In this field test we identify inadequate instructions, forms that are difficult to follow, schedules that cannot be met, and other such defects that make the course confusing to the teacher or difficult to conduct in a regular school setting. Once these deficiencies are corrected, the course is ready for commercial production.

This type of development is difficult and time-consuming.

The average Minicourse takes nearly two years to build and costs over $100,000. However, once built, it provides the school with a product they can use, and offers the user considerable evidence of course effectiveness, i.e., improvements he can expect as a result of the training.

Evaluation

A problem to which we addressed ourselves early in the conceptualization of the Minicourse model concerned the techniques that would be appropriate to determine whether our instructional materials achieved their objectives. It was obvious that the conventional methods of measuring teacher performance by global observation schedules or supervisory ratings were entirely inadequate as a device for determining whether the teacher was effectively employing specific skills in the classroom. Interaction analysis techniques, such as those developed by Flanders (1970), Medley and Mitzel (1963) and others, provided much more meaningful descriptions of the classroom situation. However, the systems that were available in 1967 had some serious limitations as tools for measuring the attainment of specific teacher performance objectives. Since these systems generally attempted to classify all teacher and pupil verbal behavior, the classifications used were too broad to provide the kind of information needed in assessing highly specific teaching skills. For example, one of the goals of Minicourse 1 was to increase the proportion of higher-order questions, as opposed to fact questions, that teachers ask during a 20-minute discussion lesson. The Flanders ten-category system has a classification (Category 4) into which all teacher questions are tallied. However, this classification does not differentiate among different types of questions and, therefore, would have to be expanded in order to be useful in measuring the questioning objectives of Minicourse 1. We encountered this same problem repeatedly in our attempts to apply available classroom interaction analysis systems to the task of measuring specific teaching performance occurring as a result of Minicourse training.*

We finally decided that the most effective way to determine whether our specific performance objectives were being achieved was to develop a special evaluation instrument for each Minicourse which focused sharply on the specific skills that the course attempted to develop. Thus, our usual method of evaluating the specific outcomes of a Minicourse is to instruct the teacher to prepare a specific type of lesson prior to starting the Minicourse. The teacher presents this lesson in his or her regular classroom and a videotape recording of the lesson is made. Near the end of the Minicourse, the teacher is given identical instructions and prepares another lesson which, in turn, is presented by the teacher and recorded on videotape. Analysis of the specific teaching behaviors on the two videotapes then provides us with evidence on the degree to which a given Minicourse achieves its objectives.

Since we are also interested in the pupil changes that occur as a result of a teachers' taking Minicourses, we collect pupil performance data in evaluating most Minicourses.

Finally, we have been concerned with the permanence of changes in teacher behavior which occur as a result of taking a Minicourse. Thus, we schedule follow-up evaluations of field test teachers in order to obtain this kind of information. For example, in the case of Minicourse 1, we collected videotape samples of the classroom performance of teachers in our main field test sample four months after and again 39 months after they had completed the course. Analysis of these follow-up tapes indicate that many of the improvements in teacher performance resulting from Minicourse 1 persist remarkably well. Teachers made significant improvement on 11 of the 13 variables measured on the pre-course and immediate post-course evaluations (Borg, 1969). Most of these changes were not only statistically significant, but were large enough to make a real difference in the way teachers conducted discussion lessons. When the four month delayed videotape was

*In his recent work (1970), Flanders proposes techniques that would provide specific performance data within the context of broad categories.

scored for the 11 significant behaviors, results indicated that teachers were still performing at the same level as their immediate post-tape performance on all but three variables. On one variable, teachers had made a significant drop, while on two others their performance had improved significantly after they had completed the Minicourse.

Even after 39 months, teacher performance was significantly above the pre-course level on eight of the ten variables that were scored. Some of the performance scores were remarkably stable over the three-year period. For example, one objective of Minicourse 1 is to increase the proportion of thought questions and reduce the proportion of fact questions teachers ask during discussion lessons. For teachers on whom all four evaluation tapes were collected, the average proportion of higher-order questions before training was .38. After the course this proportion was .50, 4 months later .51 and 39 months later .51.

A behavior that Minicourse 1 attempts to reduce is the habit many teachers have of repeating their questions. This wastes discussion time and also conditions pupils not to listen to the teacher's first statement of the question. Before taking Minicourse 1 the average teacher repeated 14.35 questions in a 20-minute discussion. Immediately after completing the course this mean was down to 5.25. The mean had dropped to 2.55 after four months and was found to be 2.50 at the 39-month follow-up.

Although we have more data on Minicourse 1 than on courses developed later, our results to date indicate that the Minicourse model has been successful in improving a wide range of teaching skills in such areas as class discussion, language instruction, mathematics tutoring, individualized instruction, role-playing, reading instruction and questioning. Within five years, we expect to have developed enough individualized learning packages so that we can provide both elementary and secondary teachers with training that will give them a broad repertoire of basic teaching skills.

References

Acheson, K.A. The Effects of Feedback from Television Recording and Three

Types of Supervisory Treatment on Selected Teacher Behavior. Unpublished doctoral dissertation, Stanford University, 1964.

Allen, D.W., D.O. Berliner, F.J. McDonald and F.T. Sobel. A Comparison of Different Modeling Procedures in the Acquisition of a Teaching Skill. Paper presented at the meeting of the American Educational Research Association, 1967.

Allen, D.W. and J.C. Fortune. An Analysis of Microteaching: New Procedure in Teacher Education. *Microteaching: A Description,* Stanford University, 1966.

Allen, D.W. and K. Ryan. *Microteaching.* Palo Alto, California: Addison-Wesley, 1969.

Bandura, A. and A.C. Huston. Identification as a Process of Incidental Learning. *Journal of Abnormal and Social Psychology,* 1961, *63,* 311-318.

Bandura, A. and C.J. Kupers. Transmission of Patterns of Self-Reinforcement Through Modeling. *Journal of Abnormal and Social Psychology,* 1963, *69,* 1-9.

Bandura, A., D. Ross and S.A. Ross. Imitation of Film-Mediated Aggressive Models. *Journal of Abnormal and Social Psychology,* 1963, *66,* 3-11.

Borg, W.R. The Minicourse as a Vehicle for Changing Teacher Behavior: The Research Evidence. Paper presented at meeting of the American Educational Research Association, 1969.

Borg, W.R., M.L. Kelley, P. Langer and M.D. Gall. *The Minicourse—A Microteaching Approach to Teacher Education.* Beverly Hills, California: Macmillan Educational Services, 1970.

Flanders, N.A. *Analyzing Teaching Behavior.* Reading, Massachusetts: Addison-Wesley, 1970.

Joyce, R.B. Personal letter to Walter R. Borg, Director, Teacher Education Program, Far West Laboratory for Educational Research and Development, July 2, 1969.

May, M.A. and A.A. Lumsdaine (Eds.). *Learning from Films.* New Haven: Yale University Press, 1958.

McDonald, F.J. A Theoretical Model for the Use of Observational Learning in Acquiring Teaching Skill. Paper presented at meeting of the American Educational Research Association, 1969.

Medley, D.M. and H.E. Mitzel. Measuring Classroom Behavior by Systematic Observation. In N.L. Gage (Ed.) *Handbook of Research on Teaching.* Rand McNally, 1963, 247-328.

Shea, J. and C. Mould. The Relative Effectiveness of Student Teaching Versus a Combination of Student Teaching and Microteaching in the Training of Teachers. Unpublished draft, University of Florida, July, 1971.

Walter R. Borg formerly Director of the Teacher Education Program of the Far West Laboratory for Educational Research and Development, is with the Department of Psychology, Utah State University, Logan.

The Life-Involvement Model
of Curriculum and Instruction

Philip G. Kapfer and Asahel D. Woodruff

The Life-Involvement Model (LIM) of Curriculum and Instruction
is a radical departure from current school practices. The LIM
places the enormously important decision-making and decision-
executing behaviors in which all people engage throughout their
lives squarely at the center of the curriculum development and
implementation effort. Through this approach, existing curriculum
and instructional practices are being attacked at their most
vulnerable points (e.g., their lack of relevance to life and
consequent motivational problems). In fact, means are being
developed that will accomplish ends just as radical as some of
those suggested by Ivan Illich in *Deschooling Society*, but without
destroying the institution that must be changed.

In the LIM, the basic phenomena of human behavior and its
change processes are used to direct curricular and instructional
decision-making and decision-execution. Although this move
introduces simplicity and clarity in educational decision-making, it
produces great difficulty in carrying out those rational decisions in
most existing schools.

Conditions for effective, meaningful and relevant learning are
hardly the hallmark of most current school systems. Drastic
changes in concepts of the roles of teachers and learners and of the
other supporting conditions for learning are essential if schools are
to seriously follow the implications of the real processes of
behavior change.

Transitional moves are necessary, but they must be planned
with great care. It is a little precarious to try to temporarily

172

combine existing school systems and the LIM without knowing the rules of safety in mixing their different chemistries. Perhaps the following examples of contrasts will help to clarify the direction of these transition moves:

Table 1

Contrasting Operational Patterns

Present Operational Patterns in Most Schools:	Operational Patterns in LIM Schools:
1. *Teaching = Learning* (Learning occurs inside a school building through primarily didactic processes.)	1. *Teaching ≠ Learning* (Learning occurs where a desired competence can be practiced with accurately perceived feedback, whether within the walls of a school building or out in the community.)
2. *Graded, K-12*	2. *Non-graded*
3. *Leveled* (Elementary, middle and high schools)	3. *Non-leveled* (K-12 in one learning community)
4. *Self-contained classrooms* (All day at the elementary level; divided into periods at the secondary level)	4. *Work stations and other areas* (Skill development areas; library and similar resource areas; chemical, physical, biological, health, mechanical, etc., areas; arts and crafts areas; social process areas for activities such as discussion sessions, planning community action programs, recreation, governance, etc.)
5. *Departmentalized content*	5. *Content within life activities*
6. *Teacher supply room*	6. *Teacher and student "parts department" or "general store"*

7. *Staffing: certificated, non-certificated* (Principal and assistants, counselors, teachers, librarians, secretaries, teacher aides, janitorial staff)

7. *Staffing: certificated, adjunct, non-certificated* (Instructional coordinator, business managers or "executive secretaries," decision-making project consultants, decision-execution project consultants, technical consultants, achievement and readiness analysts, LIM materials development specialists, school evaluation specialists)

Although operational patterns such as those suggested above in the LIM will result in a very different-looking school, they are all attainable. Most of these patterns have been demonstrated singly at one time or another, and they can all be brought together through appropriate transitional moves. Thus, the LIM does include several ideas from the past, but in a sounder psychological arrangement. These ideas, as well as the LIM itself, can be summarized as follows:

Not learning *by* doing—Learning was recognized to be dependent on doing, but was left to occur naturally without adequate planning. Hence, systematic learning suffered greatly.

Not learning *for* doing—Doing was recognized to be dependent on learning, but the learning was to occur in advance of the doing, not as an integral part of it. Because such learning was verbal in nature, it did not transfer well to functional situations.

Rather, learning *while* doing—Learning is recognized to be dependent on doing, but is deliberately planned as part of the doing process to provide both relevance and adequate scope.

Although the LIM does address itself to the standard problems and issues in curriculum, it does so from a basis of facts about human behavior and its change processes. For this reason, we will examine in the first section of this article a comprehensive model of behavior, four clearly identifiable types of behavior, and based on the above, the psychological conditions which must be present in or out of the classroom before a person's actual behavioral patterns can be arranged.

Then, in the second section of this article, we will relate this background information to the following basic curricular problems and issues:

(1) the nature of educational goals and scope of the curriculum,
(2) curriculum organization,
(3) student task pattern,
(4) individual needs and
(5) maintenance and evaluation of pupil growth and progress.

We will attempt to discuss these problems and issues as concretely as space limitations will permit so that the reader can visualize the actual operation of the LIM school and the roles of its participants.

Psychological Base for the LIM
Behavior is what people do. It runs the whole S-R range from the receiving of signals and messages from the environment, through interpretive actions, to doing something in response to them. The deceptively simple S-R formula conceals a complex array of processes that have characteristics of great importance to educational planning. When these characteristics are overlooked or misinterpreted, confusion and ineffectiveness in educational planning result.

A Comprehensive Model of Behavior
The only model of human behavior and learning that is complete enough for educational planning comes from the field of biology. The evidence from biology for this model is impressive, to say the least. It is called "psychic adaptation." *This model of the*

adaptation process is complete enough to accommodate within it, at various points in its sub-processes, all of the current psychological models of learning. Furthermore, it has the qualities of a closed cybernetic system within which we can locate *all* of the basic behavior processes that carry the burden of human learning, both in daily life outside of school and in school life.

We have taken the position, therefore, that a person is a whole organism adapting to his world (and changing that world, also). The most crucial mechanism of that adaptation process is the set of nonverbal cognitive-affective functions that result in self-formed conceptual patterns. Operant behavioral shaping and verbal storage and transmission do indeed go on within the larger process of adaptation. However, these two processes play contributing roles and not dominant roles in behavior and systematic education.

The adaptation concept of human behavior is portrayed in Figure 1. The rectangles represent the person, and the circles represent the interaction with the environment.

Four Types of Behavior

There are four types of behavior (and resulting psychological models of learning) discussed in the literature today. They are represented in Figure 2 and include (1) conditioned responses, (2) motor processes, (3) verbal processes of two kinds—reciting memorized statements and expressing thoughts and feelings and (4) conceptual-affective processes. Each of the four represents an aspect of learning, and no one of them is complete in itself. All four of these behaviors are operating simultaneously as a person moves through the man-environment interaction process shown in Figure 1. It is possible, however, to focus *educative attention* on any one of those aspects at any point in the interaction cycle.

In our view, the schools have placed primary emphasis on the verbal processes, which (because of inadequate prior or concurrent perceptual and conceptual learning) has resulted in the promotion of much memorization without understanding. Figure 2 represents spatially our view of the relative emphasis that should be placed in the educative process on the four aspects of behavior.

Figure 1

Components of the Man-Environment
Interaction Process

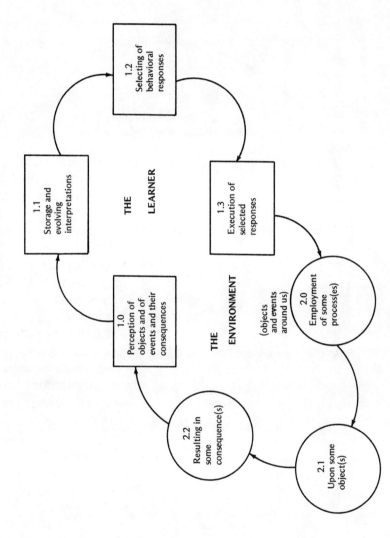

Figure 2

Estimated Relative Dominance
of the Components of Organismic Behavior

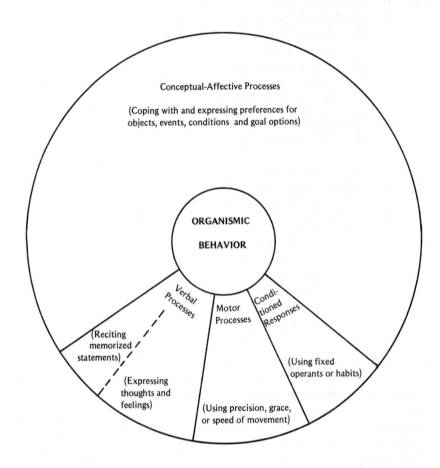

Conceptual-Affective Processes

(Coping with and expressing preferences for
objects, events, conditions and goal options)

ORGANISMIC

BEHAVIOR

Verbal
Processes

Motor
Processes

Condi-
tioned
Responses

(Reciting
memorized
statements)

(Using fixed
operants or habits)

(Expressing
thoughts and
feelings)

(Using precision, grace,
or speed of movement)

Thus, expanding on Figure 2, the important educational targets in the LIM include all of the following in psychologically appropriate relationship to each other:

1. Cognitive behavior and its affective influences.
    A. Acquiring concepts and values through direct experience.
    B. Organizing them meaningfully to serve one's motives.
    C. Acting them out in the pursuit of one's motives.
2. Verbal communicating behaviors.
    A. Memorizing the symbol systems and all of their commonly used combinations.
    B. Communicating thoughts and feelings.
3. Habit patterns (a simple and accurate term for referring to operant behaviors).
4. Motor behavior.
    A. Developing neuro-muscular coordination for countless nonskilled body movements by means of which we act upon the environment.
    B. Cultivating advanced levels of speed, grace and precision (skill) in selected body movements whose value depends on those qualities.

Conditions Necessary to Produce Behavioral Change

The behavior-change processes described so far occur constantly as an organism interacts with its environment. Unfortunately, as mentioned above, these processes have been badly distorted in the schools, particularly in those crucial areas of the curriculum upon which our personal, social, economic and political lives depend. The real environment in the school consists of teachers, examinations, dull books, academic rooms and regimented time blocks for dealing with verbal materials. It has largely excluded person-to-person interaction, social class and caste encounters, personal management of time, personal management of economic abilities and resources, civic action and leadership, and personal interdependence among citizens and neighbors in community and political life. As a consequence, students learn to handle themselves more or less well in the academic game of the school, but they do not learn how to handle themselves in the street, the neighborhood, the shop, the public forum, or in most of the other theaters of action in our society.

Behavior changes only when it is going on and when its consequences are permitted to impinge on the person behaving and on other people. This feedback serves to reinforce or extinguish the behavior. Following is a set of specifications that derive from the adaptation process:

1. A person does something overt to satisfy a want.
2. He does it in a real situation, to real things, on a "for keeps" basis.
3. The behavior is basically nonverbal and need-oriented, although the person may verbalize about it.
4. What he does involves a full cycle of behavior (shown in Figure 1):

Perceiving
Thinking and conceptual organizing
Choosing a goal and a line of
   response   With or
Executing the choice and precipi-   without
   tating a consequence   conscious
Being affected by the consequence   awareness
   and re-entering the cycle by
   perceiving some or all of those
   consequences

Curriculum Position of the LIM

In the LIM, behavior is viewed as a "coping" activity—the person makes personal decisions concerning his own behavior and participates in a series of acts consisting of manipulating concrete objects to satisfy his personal wants. This interpretation of behavior (presented in detail in the first half of this chapter) represents the psychological basis for making the curriculum decisions presented in the present section.

Consistent responses to basic curriculum problems are an

impelling need in education. For this reason, we will organize our discussion of the LIM curriculum around the five curriculum problems that were identified in the introduction to this article. In order to facilitate the discussion that follows, we have summarized in Figure 3 the curriculum position taken in the LIM.

Because the LIM is life-centered, goals consist of life behaviors (see the entry point in Figure 3). The behaviors, or goals, occur in the five areas of life. All the phenomena of the environment involved in those areas become the content with which the student becomes behaviorally familiar. Behaviors are turned into "Projects," and phenomena are turned into "Units" and "Ventures" for learning activities.

The systematic approach in Figure 3 is intended to keep goals realistic, keep content functional and instrumental to the goals, keep the learning behavior-oriented and keep evaluation faithful to the goals and immediate for its shaping value.

As shown in Figure 3, evaluation devices are constructed simultaneously with the learning activities. They are developed and operated at three levels: (1) competence in holistic life behaviors, (2) focused and instrumental learning outcomes from Units and (3) open learning outcomes of Ventures.

Nature of LIM Educational Goals and
Scope of the LIM Curriculum

All of the goals of the LIM program are centered directly on helping every learner become effective in all facets of satisfying living. Three key components of that primary goal are specified in summary fashion in Figure 4.

Issues of current critical concern such as reading, loyalty and human relations skills are accounted for in the LIM educational goals. However, such issues are not dealt with explicitly in the expanded outline of the LIM goals provided in Table 2. This is because our purpose in Table 2 is to illustrate the first two items in the materials development portion of Figure 3, namely, the "major societal goals" and the "transactions" into which those goals divide. Special areas of competence such as reading or human relations would appear at the "daily behavior" level.

Figure 3

Life-Involvement Curriculum Model

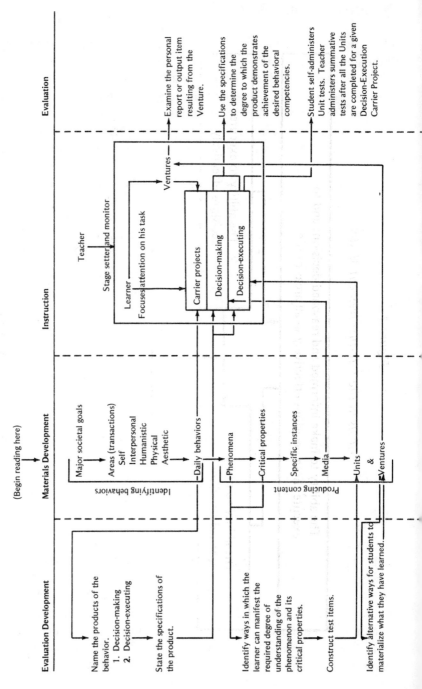

Figure 4

Goals in the Life-Involvement Model

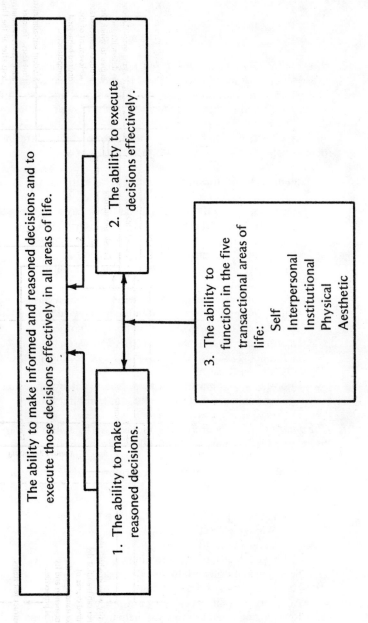

The ability to make informed and reasoned decisions and to execute those decisions effectively in all areas of life.

2. The ability to execute decisions effectively.

1. The ability to make reasoned decisions.

3. The ability to function in the five transactional areas of life:

Self
Interpersonal
Institutional
Physical
Aesthetic

Table 2

LIM Educational Goals

1. *The ability to make informed and reasoned decisions.*—The ability in
    every student to make informed and reasoned decisions about the issues
    and choices that constantly arise in his personal and social life and to
    choose goals that lead to rewarding results for himself and for others.

    In this objective, the following contributing abilities are included as
    objectives:

    > Identifying significant issues in the local, national and international
    > scene, and in one's personal life.
    > Recognizing how those issues involve and may affect himself.
    > Recognizing how those issues involve and may affect other persons.
    > Identifying values that may be preserved, enhanced or diminished
    > through personal or social actions.
    > Identifying actions he or others could or might take in various
    > situations.
    > Recognizing when learning will help in making a choice.
    > Using learning deliberately to improve knowledge about alternative
    > choices or to expand the number of choices.
    > Determining what might be required to carry out various actions.
    > Determining the probable consequences of acting in various ways in
    > a given situation.
    > Choosing a solution or goal to pursue to satisfy his wants or needs
    > and enhance preferred values for himself and others.

2. *The ability to execute decisions effectively.*—The ability in every student
    to execute his decisions and reach his goals effectively.

    In this objective, the following contributing abilities are included as
    objectives:

    > Formulating specifications for goals to be reached.
    >   Workable specifications.
    >   Creative specifications.
    > Making a job analysis for reaching a goal.
    > Selecting and using productive processes.
    > Manipulating and using materials.
    > Adapting to reality in carrying out processes.
    > Recognizing when learning will help in the pursuit of a goal.

Using learning deliberately to improve knowledge and competence.
Putting learning to immediate use in practical situations.
Evaluating personal effectiveness in doing something.

3. *The ability to function in the five transactional areas of life.*—The possession by every student of a functional comprehension of the objects and processes that make up the human environment.

In this objective, the following contributing forms of knowledge are included as objectives:

A. Himself as a responsible participant (Self Transactions). The ability to:

   (1) Consciously monitor his own daily behavior.
   (2) Set and modify his standards of values, achievement and personal ideas of right and wrong.
   (3) Set and modify his major goals for personal living and for vocational life.
   (4) Use learning deliberately as a means of succeeding in life.
   (5) Cultivate his personal appearance.
   (6) Develop his physical self.

B. Other individuals with whom he interacts (Interpersonal Transactions). The ability to:

   (1) Communicate effectively with others.
   (2) Participate in social acts.
   (3) Examine and shape his personal standards of considerateness toward others.
   (4) Consciously monitor how he treats other persons.

C. The social world and its institutions within which he lives (Institutional or Humanistic Transactions). The ability to:

   (1) Interact competently with all forms of social institutions.
   (2) Earn, save, invest and spend money competently.

D. The physical world with all of its natural laws (Physical Transactions). The ability to:

   (1) Use and consume environmental resources.
   (2) Change and produce things.

(3) Maintain, repair and service things.
(4) Transport things.
(5) Research and develop phenomena and ideas.

E. The aesthetic qualities of the world and of human life (Aesthetic Transactions). The ability to find aesthetic satisfactions in life through such behaviors as:

(1) Responding affectively to aesthetic qualities by:

Absorbing (fascinatedly consuming) a stimulus.
Identifying (imaginatively acting) with an episode laden with personal value.
Empathizing (entering into the feeling of another) in episodes charged with personal feelings.
Contemplating (imaginatively reliving one's own emotions) in relation to objects or events that impinge significantly on one's central concepts and values.

(2) Reacting cognitively to art objects by:

Describing them anecdotally.
Analyzing them.
Judging or evaluating them.

(3) Expressing aesthetic feelings by:

Producing art, music, dance, literature or drama.
Incorporating aesthetic qualities in non-art objects through designing or decorating.
Performing artistically by playing, singing, dancing, acting or oral reading.

LIM Curriculum Organization

All of the basic behaviors identified in the preceding outline of LIM goals are included in the curriculum at every maturity level. Although from time to time the relative amounts of these behaviors are distorted from their relative frequency of occurrence in life, due to the emphases that are needed at different times in a person's schooling, they all go on all the time.* For this reason, the sequence of the curriculum is from simple to complex levels of every behavior, not from one subject to another or from one behavior to another. And the depths of behavioral acts in which students engage range from global or surface acts to deeply penetrating and analytical acts (molar to molecular, or whole to part).

Student Task Pattern in the LIM

The student task pattern throughout his years in a LIM school is very much like the "informal (open) education" approach practiced in some British primary classrooms. Students report to specified areas at the beginning of the school day for planning purposes, for Glasser-type "class meetings" and for information concerning scheduled events or teamwork assignments that might be available to them that day. If they know in advance their work for the day, they then report to appropriate work stations and other areas. Or, if they need assistance in concluding or starting a project or skill development task, they report to an achievement and readiness analyst. Students move freely throughout the school building and between the school and the community, with supervision commensurate with their individual levels of self-direction and their ability to cope with potential dangers both inside and outside the school building.

As indicated above, four instructional instruments have been developed to assist students in their tasks. These instruments have received extensive field testing at all levels, beginning with

---

*Note that this is different from Bruner's statement that "any subject could be taught in some honest form to any child at any stage in his development." Bruner was talking about the verbal conceptual structure and process of disciplines and the behaviors of scholars, not the behaviors of "livers." The five-year-old entering school already exhibits musical, mathematical, scientific, social and other behaviors, even though not in a very sophisticated form. Thus, "liver" behaviors are already going on, and the school's role is to keep those behaviors going on and to provide for the perceptual, conceptual/affective, motor skill and verbal learning that increases the competency of those behaviors.

students who can use reading as a tool for learning. These four instruments have been derived from the perception, storage and interpretation, response selection and response execution behaviors shown in Figure 1. The instructional instruments are named as follows:

1. *Decision-Making Carrier Projects*—to activate response selection behaviors (1.2 in Figure 1).
2. *Decision-Execution Carrier Projects*—to activate response execution behaviors (1.3 in Figure 1).
3. *Learning Units and reference materials*—to provide functional familiarity with the critical properties of phenomena involved in Carrier Projects (1.1 in Figure 1).
4. *Ventures*—to engage students in exploring their environment in order to expand their interests and help them change their motivational states so that want-serving projects are initiated (1.0 in Figure 1).

Except for Units, which because of their complexity are typically developed by LIM materials development specialists, students soon learn to structure many of their own tasks by developing their own Carrier Projects and Ventures. Project supervisors and technical consultants provide whatever assistance is necessary as students develop and engage in such tasks. However, an extensive shelf stock of Projects, Units and Ventures should always be available to students, either for selection or for guidance in developing their own tasks.

Individual Needs

A core of daily behaviors (put in the form of Carrier Projects) and phenomena (put in the form of Ventures and Units) are engaged in by all students. The order of attack within this core, however, is individually designed. Elective choices would be made by all students in addition to the required core. Student development of his own Carrier Projects is encouraged and supported by already available or specifically designed references, Units and/or consultant help. Students also learn to develop their own Ventures. The learning activities that support a Project or a

Venture can deal with either required or optional phenomena. Many Projects, Units and Ventures are pre-prepared and available for student use at all times.

Mediation of Ventures and Units varies depending on where the phenomenon falls along a concreteness-abstractness continuum. Criteria for mediating Units and Ventures based on experimental studies in the area of concept development have been produced, and differ for concrete phenomena, generalizations and principles. Both the student and the teacher bear responsibility for determining whether or not the student has the prerequisite perceptual experience with the concrete phenomena that are represented by a generalization, including all variations within the generalization.

In the case of a principle, which is a generalized process-consequence or if-then phenomenon, the student might need to return to prerequisite Units or specific process-consequence phenomena. For example, for the principle "As its temperature increases, matter tends toward the gaseous state," the student may need prerequisite Units on molecular action and similar components of the larger phenomenon, or he may even need to have some additional experiences with basic processes and instances of heat-induced expansion. Thus, provision for individual differences and needs in the LIM is based on a determination of where the student is in his conceptual development. The kinds of phenomena and their levels of concreteness-abstractness are shown in Table 3.

Maintenance and Evaluation of Pupil
Growth and Progress in the LIM

Although the LIM instructional pattern is very much an open one, it by no means implies an unstructured environment. "Teachers" in a LIM classroom or school maintain control by (1) helping students identify behaviors that are want-serving for them—thus resulting in greatly increased motivation, (2) helping students identify or construct Carrier Projects that engage them in these want-serving behaviors in reasoned and effective ways, (3) providing for and monitoring the phenomenal learning that is necessary to accomplish the Projects, (4) providing inherently

Table 3

Kinds of Phenomena and Their Concreteness-Abstractness Levels

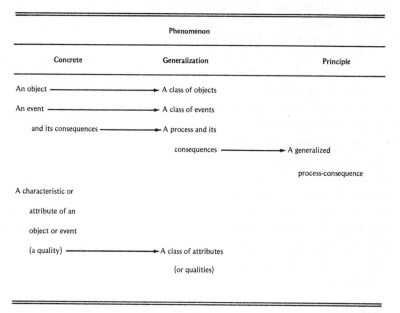

	Phenomenon	
Concrete	Generalization	Principle
An object ⟶	A class of objects	
An event ⟶	A class of events	
and its consequences ⟶	A process and its	
	consequences ⟶	A generalized
		process-consequence
A characteristic or		
attribute of an		
object or event		
(a quality) ⟶	A class of attributes	
	(or qualities)	

interesting Ventures and phenomenal materials, (5) focusing learner attention on the task rather than on the teacher, (6) eliciting highly individualistic learner responses to tasks and materials and (7) using appropriate operant conditioning techniques to establish and maintain the habit patterns that are necessary for an effective work climate. The emphasis, however, is placed on the first six of these helping behaviors. The seventh teacher behavior is looked upon as a prerequisite to establishing an environment in which the first six can go on in a productive fashion.

Record-keeping devices for keeping track of student growth and progress are important. At least two kinds of encounters are recorded. First the important daily behaviors (see Figure 3) in which learners engage are listed. The relative importance of these behaviors—in other words, priorities—are set through student, parent and community involvement and are incorporated in the devices themselves. Second the important phenomena (see Figure 3) with which students become familiar to varying depths of penetration are recorded. Given highest priority in the record-keeping system are phenomena (1) that are encountered frequently in life and (2) that require adult assistance in order for the student to acquire a behavioral understanding.

Because there are sequence patterns involved in acquiring some behavioral competencies and conceptual learnings, the record-keeping systems reflect these sequences. This facilitates teacher as well as student self-diagnosis and prescription. Because the specifications for Projects are frequently student developed, or at least altered, considerable student creativity is possible in establishing the nature of the product that is produced. The same specifications, test items and reports that are used to evaluate student attainment also would serve to evaluate the curricular materials that are used. Additional assessment methods for evaluating the total curricular and instructional system on an on-going basis are, of course, necessary for the school to remain responsive to student needs and to receive feedback from the community.

Conclusions

Several pilot efforts based on the LIM that are currently underway show great promise. In a Pilot Experimental Teacher Education Project at the University of Utah, now in its fourth year of operation, the LIM has been implemented both with University teacher-trainees and with elementary and secondary pupils in the trainees' classes. Two other projects, both of which are under the auspices of the Western States Small Schools Project, are currently implementing LIM prototype curricular materials and instructional approaches in a number of elementary and secondary schools in five western states. Affectively oriented student responses to the LIM have been overwhelmingly positive, a fact that is especially encouraging considering the transitional nature of any moves made within existing school patterns.

A very large research and development job still remains, although the procedures for carrying out most of these efforts have been designed and tested. The materials development and evaluation tasks, for example, lend themselves to several projects, ranging all the way from one-man efforts to large team and sub-team tasks. Continuing empirical research in the school setting is, of course, critical to the total engineering job. State laws, administrative policies and regulations, normative testing practices, school organization and in-service education are just a few of the supporting systems that require concerted efforts in order to fully implement the LIM in the schools.

Many of the individualized curricular materials and associated instructional procedures produced during the innovative sixties were steps in the right direction. This is especially true in those cases in which considerable emphasis was given to student self-initiative and responsibility and in which the student's primary focus of attention was transferred from the teacher to the learning task. However, these moves toward curriculum innovation have not been sufficient to solve the serious motivational problems that exist in an essentially verbalistic approach. Such problems cannot be solved by combining curricular innovations that were derived without reference to the psychological facts that operate in adaptive learning. Rather, what is needed is a complete rebuilding from the ground up, based on the facts of the man-environment adaptive process, of both the curriculum and the way in which schools operate.

Philip G. Kapfer and **Asahel D. Woodruff** are on the staff of the Bureau of Educational Research, University of Utah, Salt Lake City.

Discovery Boxes

Rebecca Corwin

The curriculum kits most recently developed at the Children's Museum in Boston, Massachusetts, are called "Discovery Boxes." They differ somewhat from the other units developed at the Museum, and perhaps a review of the different types will point up their similarities, differences and some evolution in our thinking about loan materials for the classroom.

The initial units developed for loan from the museum were kits of artifacts loosely collected about a central title or theme, such as "Dolls from Other Lands," "The Circus," or "France." These came in part from the Museum collections and in part from materials collected by donors and museum personnel. Each box included an assortment of three-dimensional materials, pictures, graphs, pamphlets and maps for illustrative purposes. They were intended for use as display collections, with some handling by children. Use was largely left up to the teacher.

Because of some feeling that these collections of materials, although useful, were of limited value for teaching in-depth concepts, kits called MATCH units (*M*aterials and *A*ctivities for *T*eachers and *Ch*ildren) were developed in the mid- and late sixties, through a federal grant. These were much more extensive kits of real materials, books and films built around specific whole-class and group activities. Units were structured to last for two to three weeks, and careful lesson plans and background materials were included in the teachers' guides. Topics ranged from "Netsilik Eskimos" to "Rocks" to "Medieval People" to "A House of Ancient Greece."

193

Two new kinds of loan boxes grew from the MATCH units. One, the Mini-MATCH unit, was similar in concept to the MATCH unit, but dealt with a smaller piece of learning.

The fourth type, and the latest in the series, is the Discovery Box. Five of these are in circulation now, with more planned. A typical kit consists of a teacher's guide, which includes information about the kit and materials, some suggestions on how to start, book suggestions, follow-up activities, and extensions of learning into other areas of the curriculum. The kit itself is designed around a concept, such as printing, and contains materials for a small group of children to work independently of the teacher. In the Discovery Box on printing, for example, stamp pads, a re-inker and objects with which to print, such as alphabet stamps, geometric-shape stamps, natural-shape stamps and rolling stamps are included. Most of the stamps are carved from rubber erasers, and provide ideas for children and teachers for finding their own printing objectives. Thus, the class is encouraged to continue the theme beyond the kit rental time by making their own materials.

From this brief description, it is obvious that no matter what the subject of the kit, real objects for children to touch are included. This approach coincides with the basic belief of the Museum that children learn from touching and manipulating, and from making the kinds of connections that physical involvement can provide. As much as possible, also, illustrative material is provided so that materials are used and activities take place within a context that helps a child to interpret and extend his learning.

Developing the Discovery Box

Many of the boxes are tried out with children and adults who visit the museum. Development is done in groups, in which developers spend their time in trying materials as children might. Extensions to learnings, activity ideas and further development are also frequently gathered by the use of materials from the kits with classroom teachers. Since one of our basic tenets is that children do in fact learn through purposeful play, the developers frequently "play," watching themselves and each other as to the learnings which emerge. It is our conviction that it is impossible to specify or guarantee *one* learning outcome from *any* experience for a large group of children. Instead, we can suggest some probable outcomes for children, and must leave evaluation of learning up to the classroom teacher. If, for instance, one classroom produced and bound a book using the "Printing" Discovery Box, and another spent the bulk of their time making patterns with various letters, the learnings would be significantly different, although not completely so. We also test materials to make sure that they are intrinsically interesting to children and that real discovery is possible. Many of the suggested activities have grown from children as they have used the materials, with little or no direction.

Uses of Discovery Boxes

Recent educational thinking has tended to lead us away from teacher-dominated learning and into increasing independence on the part of the child. Thus, we provide job cards giving suggestions to or posing questions for the child. It is our conviction that children must have the opportunity to explore materials and their possibilities, but that most productive exploration happens within a framework. Thus, each Discovery Box begins with a structured activity that has closure, that allows a child to learn something about the materials provided and that will provide a stepping-off point both for children who will then continue on their own quite independently and for others, who will continue to function in response to job card suggestions. For example, the "Bulbs and Batteries" kit gets children started with the standard first problem of getting a bulb to light using one battery and one piece of wire. Then the cards continue through a sequence of nine problems, which get increasingly complex (but which do not need to be done in order). We have found, however, that after the first problem, many children simply proceed through their own problems, trying out different combinations of bulbs, switches, bells and wiring patterns. Thus, we try to provide for both learning styles—the "linear learner" and the "messer-about."

A growing conviction that "messing about" is necessary has led us to providing for both of these learning styles. We feel that both approaches are best done in small groups with some guidance. We try to provide experiences which are both simple and complex, structured and at the same time open-ended, and within which children will share with each other their learnings as they work on their own solutions to problems. In typical schools and districts, it is nearly impossible for a teacher to provide enough opportunities for children to come into contact with and work with real materials. Borrowing kits from a place like the museum can give the teacher the opportunity to observe his children learn with new things and to extend the learnings from those materials into other areas of the curriculum. Therefore, we have worked hard to make the teachers' guides effective, by giving many suggestions of books, activities and other materials for follow-up to the kinds of learnings started by these discovery kits.

Schools largely deny the child the opportunity to follow an interest through many of its extensions. A sensitive teacher, given enough support through provision of both materials and ideas, can feel more confident in encouraging the taking apart of a flashlight to see how it works, dismantling an old mixer for the same purpose, trying to wire a flashing light that signals when a door is open. It is through this kind of experience that a child learns and retains his knowledge. A fair evaluation of that sort of retention is to ask a child to try a solution to an analogous problem. If he can make the connection, he's definitely "got it."

We have tried in all cases to make the Discovery Box (or any of our other kits, for that matter) stand completely on its own. All teacher training takes place through the manual. In borrowing one of the kits, the teacher needs nothing but what is provided. The reasons for this lie largely with our desire to have teachers relax and look at children's learning in a different way than they normally do. Because the Discovery Boxes run themselves, except for clean-up and various stimuli on the part of the teacher, it is our hope that teachers will be encouraged to make available to children more of this kind of exploratory group work with materials.

Because we see Discovery Boxes as seeds, giving teachers and children opportunities to learn in different ways, and as models of what some teacher-made kits might be like, we do not intend them for specific teaching of curriculum content, at least as most curricula now stand. Curricula should, rightly, grow from certain sorts of activities (weighing, measuring, mixing, printing, sorting), from certain developmental needs on the part of children (classifying, describing, talking, building) and from certain materials (water, buttons, sand, colored liquids, wood), when sensitively mediated by an adult who knows those children's individual learning needs and styles. Therefore, formal curricula, although sometimes useful as a jumping-off point, frequently serve to get in the way of extending learning, and often hamper a teacher's ability to provide valuable learning for each child operating in his own best learning style. We do not see learning as a linear progression, nor do all children learn best that way. Some do, and for those a sequence, job cards which progress in difficulty, or a workbook, are all to the good. For others, however, the opportunity to follow interests in an independent style is essential. That is what discovery and Discovery Boxes are all about.

Rebecca Corwin is Resource Center Director, Children's Museum, Boston, Massachusetts.

An Instructional System Conducive to Humanism: CEMREL's Aesthetic Education Program

Stanley S. Madeja

If one values humanism as an element in the educational process, an element not only to be maintained at its present level, but to be augmented, how is this to be accomplished within the ongoing movement toward increased systematization and technology?

One answer is inherent in the nature of the aesthetic experience as defined for the Aesthetic Education Program of CEMREL, Inc., a regional educational laboratory. The laboratory has had as its major concern the development of instructional systems. These systems have been directed toward the areas of early childhood education, mathematics and aesthetic education. Among these three, the Aesthetic Education Program offers a unique opportunity to evolve an instructional resource which is humanistic in its substantive base.

"An aesthetic experience is an experience which is valued intrinsically, an experience which is valued for itself."[1] That is, the aesthetic experience is a phenomenon valued without rewards other than itself. Such an experience can never be forced within the framework of extrinsic rewards. Such stimuli as have been used to encourage learning in the past—money, status, approval, fear—are outside the realm of aesthetic experience. And any system giving guarantees or token rewards must also be considered outside that realm. This is not to say that the offering of resources in aesthetic experience is something beyond any method of instruction. Because this is so, a resource for aesthetic education which is conceptually sound, and carefully planned and utilized may be a significant means of insuring a humanistic input to the educational process.

All of this, then, leads to three additional questions: Can an instructional system be developed consistent with the nature of the aesthetic experience and within which resources for aesthetic education can be offered? Can this system allow some degree of flexibility and choice for students and their communities? And, finally, can such a system be compatible with all of the above and still be pedagogically sound and substantively based?

An Instructional System for Developing Resources for Aesthetic Education

A paper by Madeja and Kelly[2] outlines an instructional system for the development of an aesthetic education curriculum commensurate with the ideal stated above. Two areas of concern are important in implementing a system for developing a resource base for aesthetic information. First, there is the area of how content is selected and organized.

The instructional system described by Madeja and Kelly is divided into content groupings which are built around centers of attention. The materials for the primary grades are divided into four groupings: Introduction to Aesthetic Phenomena, Elements in the Arts Disciplines and the Environment, The Process of Transformation and People in the Arts. Such centers of attention are possible focal points for student activities in aesthetic education and are representative of aesthetic phenomena and the relationships among them. There is an attempt to define the parameters of each center of attention so as to have continuity among packages within a grouping. For example, the roles of professionals in the arts are all similar in that each is concerned with the process of transforming an idea into a finished work of art. Thus, the materials and activities for packages in grouping four, People in the Arts, are constructed with this in mind.

The first grouping, Introduction to Aesthetic Phenomena, investigates the aesthetic qualities of time, space, motion, sound and light. These elements transcend the arts disciplines and thus provide a means for unifying studies of the arts into aesthetic education. Exemplars from all the arts disciplines form the content for this series. A basic premise in each of the units is that all phenomena, whether man-made or natural, *may* have aesthetic qualities.

In the second groupings, Elements in the Arts Disciplines and the Environment, the center of attention encompasses concepts that relate specifically to the elements utilized in the arts and the environment, such as texture in music, shape in the visual arts, movement in dance. The emphasis is on recognition of the element within an arts discipline and its relationship to the structure of the whole work. Although the student is engaged in activities which are transforming this element into an art form, the emphasis is more on perceiving and describing the element's structure and examining its function in the creative process in order to begin development of the critical and descriptive skill necessary in making aesthetic judgments.

The third center of attention, The Process of Transformation, presents methods of organizing the elements through the creative process, or the process of transforming the elements into whole works of art. The student is attending to methods by which he creates his own structure and, in the process, creates works of art. Thus, he enters into the process of making aesthetic judgments. Inherent in this is the formulation of a basis for aesthetic judgments by the students.

People in the Arts, the fourth center of attention, emphasizes how professionals in the arts organize arts elements into the whole work. The continuity in this group is based on the role similarities that all artists share within the creative process—each originates an idea and organizes elements into an end product that communicates. Several patterns begin to emerge in packages of this group. Although artists may work in different disciplines utilizing different materials and methodologies, the structures of their works and the process of transformation exhibit similarities. This last center of attention represents an important cross-pollination. Through the artist's role, students experience exemplary implementation of the other three centers of attention.

The centers of attention or contents are translated into the activities, and the activities elicit student behaviors. These behaviors—to analyze, to judge, to perceive, to produce-perform, to react, to talk and to value—categorize the types of student outcomes for the packages. In formulating these outcomes, there was much discussion as to whether or not a hierarchy among the behaviors should be created to specify program outcomes at specific educational levels. However, it became clear that any narrow ordering of behaviors by level would be artificial in light of the extensive overlapping of behaviors in each package.

As a result of this development process, behaviors which are specifically stated in each package evolved into three categories: *stimulus behaviors,* those which introduce the student to the content of the packages; *means behaviors,* through which the student interacts with the content of the package; and *end behaviors,* those which indicate learning of the content of the package. These categories are adopted from Reimer's summary of aesthetic behaviors.[3]

Although the packages are not sequenced, they are placed in groups according to content, providing school administrators with resource material from which to build a course of study in aesthetic education for a school. The arrangement of packages into sequences of learning experiences is thus left to those who know the school's policies and population best. In addition, there is overlapping between the series, which will provide the necessary linkages for eventual sequencing of packages into extended segments of instruction by grade level.

The task of developing alternative maps for sequencing the packages will be an ongoing process during the development of the entire Aesthetic Education Program. Information will be gathered to facilitate this process in the extended pilot testing described in the next section of this report. These will be termed approaches to study or alternative models for instruction.

The Development Process

In the early stages of the program the set of guidelines which provided a theoretical and content base for packages were developed.[4] Ideas were further refined by the staff associates,[5] experts in each of the arts and psychology, who developed content outlines in their respective disciplines. Topics were then defined for the packages and the development process initiated with the curriculum writer exploring in a classroom his ideas for a package. It is here that the artist, now curriculum developer, has an opportunity to get immediate reactions from children on the effectiveness of the material or idea. Frequently these children catch the essence of the educational experience in such a way that the kinds of materials are determined by the very type of child who will be using them. The process used in developing these units follows a development model which is based on a systems approach.

It should be noted that this cycle is repeated for each package of materials. During the initial phase of prototype development, outcomes are stated, activities are suggested, teacher-student learning instructions are written and the supporting materials are specified. Attention is also given to assessing the effect of the materials upon the students. At all important points in the development process, the artist-writers and the evaluation team try out a package or parts of a package with students in a

Figure 1

Stages of Materials Development

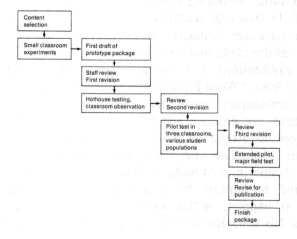

classroom situation, and these classroom trials provide the means for continuous revision of the materials. When a package is sufficiently developed, it is given to a classroom teacher who is willing to teach the entire package in sequence to his class. During this time, the students' and teacher's reactions are carefully observed so that further revisions can be made to ready the materials for pilot testing on a wide range of students in a variety of school settings.

Extended pilot tests of the initial packages are now being conducted on a national population and are presently in eight states and thirty-one school districts. This experience provides for the testing and revision of the materials on the basis of actual classroom experiences based on reactions of teachers and students and observations and data collected. Hence, the schools and the students are the laboratory, and the staff works within this context continually throughout the development process. Eventually, the materials will be turned over to a commercial publisher, after the AEP Staff has satisfied themselves that the materials are stable and after they have sufficient evidence that they are indeed a positive addition to the instructional resource of the school.

It is estimated that approximately ten packages, or one hundred hours of instruction per level, will be provided by these four series of packages for the primary grades. The content of the packages varies according to the series in which the packages are included. In two representative examples of Aesthetic Education Program packages, student involvement with the materials is largely self-directed, and the teacher is left free to encourage further explorations and reinforce important concepts on an individual basis. "Word Pictures" introduces the idea that, through precise combination, words define or expand meaning, and that the student can produce and perceive new verbal images. He is encouraged to attend to the flexibility of language and to his power to manipulate and make judgments about language. The package enables him to build skills in combining words and, at the same time, to improve his ability to perceive the thing that is defined—or happens—within a variety of specific combinations or contexts. His behaviors create a method of working like that of a poet or writer. In "Dramatic Plot" the student manipulates game-like materials in order to gain an understanding that dramatic plot, a major element in theater, is the selection and arrangement of the incidents, crisis, resolution, setting, characters and conflict in a theater experience. He is then asked to use these elements to create his own plot for a dramatic presentation and has an opportunity to analyze the structure of his own composition.

To put the development effort into perspective, the Aesthetic Education Program is now concentrating on the instructional materials resource outlined in the figure which follows. Yet to be completed is the task of developing "Approaches for Study for Aesthetic Education" where specific criteria related to a school, or schools, and groups of students can be applied. This task will be accomplished as the primary programs come to completion.

Conclusions and Summary

Since the instructional system described here has not been conceived of as *a* curriculum, but as a resource for the development of curricula, it is often thought of as lacking a rationale, since specified behavioral outcomes over a long term have not been established yet with any specificity. However, since we are not proposing the Aesthetic Education Program for a single school district, geographical area or socioeconomic group, it is necessary that the accumulative outcome would be relative to how the school finally organizes the content. For example, if a school system prefers a traditional curriculum with activities and stated outcomes, a rigid scope and sequence of the materials could be organized.

However, the important point is that it is not *mandatory* to follow a traditional table of organization. There are alternative ways of using the materials, and there are alternate ways of organizing them. Therein lies the unique aspect of the program, giving it applicability to all schools and all students. This has to be preserved in the program if the integrity of the individual is to be kept as a control on the system. The diverse nature of aesthetic experience must be presented so as to reflect alternative concep-

Figure 2*

The Foundation for the Aesthetic Education Curriculum Program
Showing Levels of Planning and Components of Units of Instruction

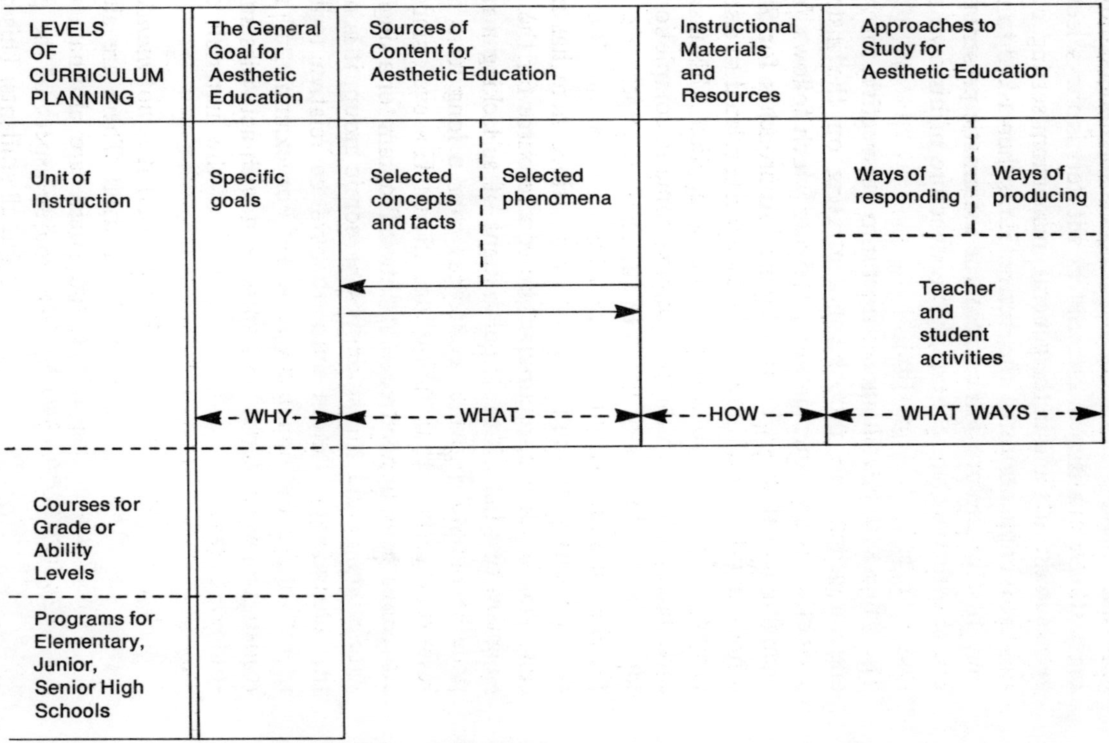

LEVELS OF CURRICULUM PLANNING	The General Goal for Aesthetic Education	Sources of Content for Aesthetic Education		Instructional Materials and Resources	Approaches to Study for Aesthetic Education	
Unit of Instruction	Specific goals	Selected concepts and facts	Selected phenomena		Ways of responding	Ways of producing
					Teacher and student activities	
Courses for Grade or Ability Levels						
Programs for Elementary, Junior, Senior High Schools						
	-- WHY --	-- WHAT --		-- HOW --	-- WHAT WAYS --	

*Barkan, Chapman and Kern, Guidelines: Curriculum Development for Aesthetic Education, CEMREL, Inc., 1970, p. 9.

tions of the phenomena. This cannot be accomplished without applying concepts and facts that reflect diverse ways of experiencing aesthetic qualities in encounters with a variety of objects and events in the arts and in the general environment.

The implications of the Aesthetic Education Program are not only that we are providing a resource for instruction in the school, but also that we are contemplating that the schools' value system may change by the insertion of this content into the curriculum. The value systems which are operating now in the communities and the schools are probably not as receptive to the content in aesthetics as to other areas of study. However, this situation is changing and that is why this program seems to be for the "now" school and the future rather than something for a decade ago. This program has the potential of being a catalyst not only for introducing more aesthetic content into the school system and introducing a feeling of joy into the learning experience, but also for changing the attitudes of the school and community regarding what education should be.

This is not a utopian plan, but one which we think is in the vanguard of what instructional systems for school should be. Such systems should provide a method for organizing their own resources rather than adopting an established organizational structure. It is imperative that the individuals who are involved with students and the students themselves have, in the words of the technocrats, "input into the system." These criteria are important from a humanistic view and they are important from a realistic view in terms of what is happening to schools and students today.

Notes

1. Manuel Barkan, Laura H. Chapman and Evan J. Kern. *Guidelines: Curriculum Development for Aesthetic Education* (St. Louis: CEMREL, Inc.) June, 1970, p. 7.
2. Stanley S. Madeja and Harry T. Kelly. A Curriculum Development Model for Aesthetic Education, *The Journal of Aesthetic Education,* IV (April, 1970), 53-63.
3. Bennett Reimer. Aesthetic Behaviors in Music. *Toward an Aesthetic*

Education (Washington, D.C.: Music Educators National Conference and St. Louis: CEMREL, Inc.), 1971, pp. 65-87.
4. Manuel Barkan, Laura H. Chapman and Evan J. Kern. *Guidelines: Curriculum Development for Aesthetic Education* (St. Louis: CEMREL, Inc.).
5. Staff Associates: John Cataldo, David Ecker, Brian Hansen, Reid Hastie, Alma Hawkins, Alan Purves, Bennett Reimer and Asahel Woodruff.

Stanley S. Madeja is Director, Aesthetic Education Project, Central Midwestern Regional Educational Laboratory, Inc., St. Ann, Missouri.

A Taxonomy for Decision-Making in Individualized Instruction

Donald T. Tosti and N. Paul Harmon

In a recently developed model for the teaching-learning process (Tosti and Ball, 1969), the three major functions present in any teaching system are described. An analysis of this model shows that the quality of an educational system depends upon:

1. The quality of presentation and display.
2. The nature and extent of student participation.
3. The accuracy of decisions regarding the assignment of the most appropriate learning activities for a student considering his needs, abilities, aspirations and motivations.

To date most innovations in education have been primarily concerned with the first function. Films, educational television, typical audio-visual devices and even team teaching are examples of this. Student participation has received attention to a lesser degree. Many new curricula have been designed to involve the student in more problem-solving and laboratory activities, but only recently have there been any attempts at improving the precision of instructional decisions. A truly effective educational system must provide all three of these necessary functions.

It is probable that a revolution in the quality of education will come not from the availability of new media nor the introduction of any specific kinds of devices, like the computer or teaching machine, although these will in their way contribute. Instead, it will come from the increased application of the growing body of knowledge about the form, purpose and processes involved in decision-making in the classroom. The term for this development is *instructional management.* Although many of the principles of instructional management have been well established for years, it is only recently, with the introduction of programmed instruction and individualized learning systems, that a systematic analysis of learning decisions has been undertaken. Instructional management can be defined as *those activities involved in the decision to initiate a specific activity for a given student, based upon the assessment of some behavior of that student.* One of the most common examples of instructional management occurs when the instructor, ascertaining that a student is having difficulty learning a particular skill, decides to assign special homework or to provide individual tutoring. The general logic of this activity, that is, *assessing behavior* → *selecting presentation* → *initiating a new activity,* can be extended from this simple situation to provide the base for rules employed in most new programs of individualized instructional systems and computer-managed classrooms.

Individualized Instruction Defined

In the principles of instructional management, a distinction between individualized and nonindividualized instruction can be made. This distinction should not be made on the basis of whether a hundred students are experiencing the same learning activity at the same time, since it is possible that every one of them *should* be engaged in this activity at this time. Nor should the distinction be made on the basis of whether or not the instructional system allows a student to progress at his own pace, as a book can. Instead, the degree of individualization must be defined in terms of instructional management. This means that:

Individualized instruction is a function of the frequency with which the decision to change the instructional presentation is made as a result of the assessment of an individual student's achievements, needs or aspirations.

The presence of large groups in an instructional setting tends to inhibit the individualization process due to the logistics of data collection, processing, assigning and so forth. Still, limited individualized instruction occurs in almost every classroom. When an instructor stops to modify his presentation as a function of a student's query, that student (but not the others who are in the room) is receiving a form of individualized instruction.

Even in a highly individualized instructional system, some group work is appropriate. For example, after some assessment, we may determine that fifty students require a given film or lecture which may be most economically delivered at a particular time, with no loss of effectiveness.

Individualization constitutes a continuum, based upon the frequency at which decisions to assess repertoire and modify presentation are undertaken—in short, the frequency at which the management of instruction occurs. Since individualization is a continuum, all we can say is that one program is more individualized than another.

A human tutor also provides a highly individualized program. The Socratic method involves a constant demand for student response in order for the tutor to determine whether or not the preceding presentation produced the desired learning effect. If not, the tutor presents an alternative explanation of the concept.

The Role of Independent Study

Self-instruction is *not* synonymous with individualized instruction. It is possible to give every student a programmed instruction (PI) text, tell them to go away and work on it, return when they are finished, and take a final examination. But, if that is all we did, we would not have gone very far along the continuum of individualization from that afforded by conventional lecture programs. Other independent study programs, such as the audio-tutorial method or correspondence courses, are no more individualized than PI, if the students all receive the same presentation, regardless of their needs.

However, independent study programs may permit more individualization than lecture systems, simply because the student can usually initiate more remedial action on his own, that is, he can choose to re-read the PI or the correspondence text, or replay the audio-tutorial tapes. In a lecture situation he has no opportunity to "replay" the instructor; the best he can do is to read his notes. Thus, to the extent that the student can repeat segments of the material, some degree of individualization is inherent in an independent study program.

Such programs have often produced better results than conventional lectures, not because of the degree of individualization provided but because they have been empirically tested and revised. Hence the quality of the display is increased. Probably more importantly, such programs demand considerably more student participation than do conventional programs.

In most cases, however, the independent study aspect of a system may be a trivial consideration in terms of the learning process. The primary effects of self-instruction are logistical and motivational. It is logistically important because it frees the instructor from the constraints of acting as an information display device and allows him to engage in instructional management relevant to the individualization process. Obviously, individualization may occur whether the materials are self-paced or not, if sufficient resources are available to allow the instructor to lecture and also permit him to perform instructional management functions.

Motivational considerations of self-pacing are very real but are not yet well documented. Several studies have indicated that when asked what aspects of an individualized program students most like, the response "going at your own rate" is usually singled out.

A Taxonomy for Individualization

So far we have primarily discussed individualization to provide for remediation. There are several other possible forms of individualization, each of which has its own data-decision rules as to what form of student characteristic we are attending to, and what kinds of actions are available. The form of individualization that we have dealt with so far in this article has been termed "achievement management." Achievement management procedures are designed to assure that the students achieve the objectives of the course. The types of learning outcomes we have discussed so far are those that could be evaluated by some type of objective or essay test. We are not limited only to objective evaluation, but the more subjective the evaluation, the greater the requirement for expert knowledge on the part of the person doing the evaluation. This usually implies that the instructor handle all such evaluations himself.

It is evident that the three elements of instructional management (repertoire assessment, selection decision, and initiation of new activity) can vary in their composition, depending on the purpose of management. We have isolated seven purposes that may be achieved. We feel these purposes can form a structure for eventual development of a taxonomy of Instructional Management Strategies:

1. *Aspiration Management.* Purpose: To select those objectives required to meet a given student's aspirations or interest.

2. *Achievement Management.* Purpose: To ensure that the student has mastered the objective specified.

3. *Prescriptive Management.* Purpose: To ensure that a given student receives the materials appropriate to his individual characteristics to best meet the objectives.

4. *Motivation Management.* Purpose: To ensure alert and continual student interaction with the educational stimuli in order to increase individual learning rates and performance levels.

5. *Enrichment Management.* Purpose: To provide for access to additional information relevant to the objectives but not necessary for their attainment.

6. *Maintenance Management.* Purpose: To ensure long-term maintenance of the student's continuing ability to perform at a pre-specified criterion level.

7. *Support Management.* Purpose: To ensure that such data be collected as necessary to keep the instructional system operating effectively and to provide individuals outside the system with information they require to evaluate and revise the existing instructional system.

Each of these types of instructional management has implications for both instructional design specialists and supervisors of existing systems.

The consideration of each of these types of instructional management and the degree to which they are formally dealt with varies greatly in existing programs. For example, few programs deal with motivation on a formal basis, but most systems provide for some kind of remediation and therefore produce some form of achievement management.

Achievement Management

Achievement management is by far the most common form of instructional management. It may occur whenever a student "error" is detected, and its purpose is to remedy such errors. The lecturer who suddenly realizes from student questions that his lecture has been "over their heads" has taken the first step in achievement management. If he now modifies his presentation to remedy those misunderstandings, he has performed an act of achievement management.

After a student has interacted with an instructional presentation, it is appropriate to determine if he has acquired the information contained in that presentation. This "check" on mastery and the subsequent decisions for remediation define another form of achievement management.

Bloom *et al.* (1971) propose the use of what they call "formative evaluation procedures" for making instructional decisions. In their analysis, they ascribe two separate functions to formative evaluation. These are:
1. To act as feedback to students as to their progress.
2. To locate student errors for the initiation of remedial assignments.

In our analysis of achievement management, we contend that the first function may be considered a specific case of the second, i.e., the primary effect of feedback is to act as a stimulus for the student to take some action of self-remediation. From this definition, it is evident that the procedures for formative evaluation form a sub-set of achievement management strategies.

Aspiration Management

Aspiration Management is concerned with the selection of sets of objectives which will allow a student to achieve a desired goal. Such a goal may be long range or may reflect very short-lived interests.

Many researchers feel that some form of aspiration management is a necessary condition for individualized instruction. The authors believe, however, that it is erroneous to conclude that because any one form of instructional management is absent from a given system, the system is not individualized. Nevertheless, we have noted that some of our colleagues emphatically deny that a given instructional system is "truly" individualized if it omits a particular form of instructional management. It seems that each management form has its patrons.

Prescriptive Management

It is a waste of resources as well as an imposition on the student to force all students through the same learning experiences. There are many individual differences among students, and the more such differences are used to prescribe instruction, the greater the *efficiency* of the system.

The most frequently used form of prescriptive management involves the use of data from achievement pretests to determine proper curriculum placement. This form of prescription allows the teacher to assign certain instructional units, exercises, or supplementary activities to the learner, based on his pretest scores, the teacher's knowledge of the materials and the knowledge of the learner's past performance.

Prescriptive management strategies for curriculum placement vary in their complexities. The most elementary form can be seen in the "skip ahead, if you know this material" options given in many programmed instruction courses.

A form of prescriptive management frequently proposed, but seldom delivered, is that which is designed to accommodate various learning styles.

The general strategy for such forms of prescriptive management involves analyzing a given student's behavioral profile prior to instruction in order to predict what the most appropriate instructional path for him would be. This "ideal path" would be designed to allow him to achieve the objective in the most efficient manner possible.

In practice, however, an achievement management strategy is usually substituted for this type of prescriptive management. Students are forced through a given learning experience; and, if they fail to meet the objectives, one of the standard strategies of achievement management is used to remedy their difficulties. To obscure the fact that what is delivered is not what was promised, the assignment given is often called the "prescription."

Motivation Management

No matter how good a learning system is, if we can't keep the student in the learning environment and responding at a satisfactory pace, the system will fail. One solution is to build motivational activities into instructional systems that ensure that the student's learning activities lead to some positive consequence. Such a concept is in perfect agreement with laboratory studies on reinforcement, which typically use the positive consequence of eating or drinking to motivate behavior. Although equivalent kinds of reinforcement have been used with students, such payoffs are usually impractical in classroom use. Students cannot be starved, nor can candy be placed in their mouths for correct responses. There are, however, many other kinds of preferred activities that can be employed in the classroom.

One formal administrative technique employed to provide positive consequences for activities has been termed "contingency management." In some programs, students "contract" for rewards. Student contracts for reinforcing activity have been used in settings varying from preschool to college.

A variation of the contingency management approach is the establishment of a token or micro-economy. In such systems, satisfactory performance leads to the deliverance of "points" or tokens which can later be used to "buy" desirable objects or activities.

Many individualized systems that employ some form of achievement management impose a "mastery contingency," e.g., the student must achieve 90 percent of the objectives of a section before he is allowed to progress to the next segment. A number of researchers have pointed out that this clearly establishes a strong motivational contingency. It is interesting to speculate that while most proponents of individualized instruction emphasize the prescriptive and remedial decisions made in their programs, it is quite possible that the motivational management component introduced by the mastery contingency is the most important factor in the success of such programs.

Enrichment Management

Enrichment involves the selection of materials that are related to the basic core content, but which either go into more depth or present interesting sidelights into core concepts. Some reasons given for enrichment management are that it acts as a time filler, aids to motivate the student, provides for greater generalization and so forth. This type of management will undoubtedly become more important as systems become more refined. At the moment it usually exists not by plan but because system objectives are so vague that instructors are uncertain whether or not a particular module is necessary to the achievement of a particular set of objectives.

Maintenance Management

Few existing instructional systems take upon themselves the task of assuring that the student will be able to recall important information or continue to maintain a skill after he has left the formal learning environment.

Maintenance management often implies that some counseling/decision-making functions be provided for the student who is preparing to leave the instructional system. The student should be advised as to future courses he should take to maintain his present skill level. Or, it may be that he should learn particular exercises to be performed at a certain frequency if his skills are to remain sharp.

The instructional system that does not concern itself with maintenance of the student's repertoire is perhaps admitting that its subject matter is simply knowledge to be acquired and then promptly forgotten.

Support Management

Some data naturally arise from any system (e.g., student time, number of instructors or aides required to keep the system running, mean final exam scores, etc.) and other data can be collected with a certain amount of effort.

Some of these data may be used to make decisions in the operational system to provide logistic support relevant to materials availability, scheduling, administrative grading and maintenance of the operating facilities.

Other data may serve as inputs to a separate Curriculum Development and Revision system. Obviously, there must be some reasonable trade-off between how much classroom manager effort should be allotted to gathering data that are irrelevant to present students and the need to have such data to help change curricula to help future students. There is no easy answer to this problem; however, the computer may soon make the gathering of data such a simple task that the classroom manager need not concern himself with it.

Media Employed in Instructional Management

For purposes of classification, we may define an *educational medium* as *any device capable of processing, storing and transmitting information within the instructional system*. We can then describe a class of media whose primary function is instructional management.

Instructional Management Media are devices involved in determining in what activities the student should engage. These devices may be classified into three sub-groups:

1. *Assessment Media*—Grade and/or reduce data concerning student responses.
2. *Decision Media*—Compare the processed data to a set of criteria to make decisions regarding future student assignments.
3. *Initiation Media*—Activate the assigned activities.

The following are Instructional Management Media:

Instructor Management. The instructor is obviously a flexible and potent management medium, but giving individual assignments to each of thirty students within present classroom constraints usually is not practical. This difficulty can be mitigated by the introduction of some of the new display media which free the instructor from the normal role as a dispenser of information, to give him more time to manage the educational environment. There are also trends toward differentiated staffing which would allow teacher aides or paraprofessionals to perform some of the supporting activities.

Computer Management. Computers may be totally or partially substituted for the instructor within the management function. In the limited case, the computer would perform only the function of assessment (grading and reducing the data). The instructor would still make the assignment decisions and initiate the activities.

Proctor Management. Although the computer has stirred the greatest interest, it obviously is not the only non-instructor management medium that can be used. By far the most widely used of these media are the teacher aides or proctors. The proctors are usually more advanced students or sometimes peers. In such systems, the aides are used primarily as assessors, but are sometimes involved in the decision function and less frequently as initiators.

Student Management. We often overlook the fact that the student himself can assess much of the data and make his own decisions. These decisions may require only minimal guidance from the teacher (or from a computer). For example, the student views the presentation, makes his response, and the teacher assesses it. We now have at least an appropriate learning sequence to remedy any deficiencies; or he can provide the student with the assessed data and allow him to initiate his own achievement management (error correction) behavior.

Conclusion

In this paper, we have taken an approach that may be considered opposite from that usually used in defining an individualized instructional system. Typically, individualized instruction is defined in terms of the resources employed; for example, the integrated use of media, the use of proctors, self-paced materials and so forth. We instead define individualized instruction in terms of its *impact on the learner, specifically in terms of the frequency of the decision to change instructional presentations as a result of assessing student behavior.* This approach increases our analytical power in two directions: first, by providing a system for developing a taxonomy of strategies which can be used to accomplish individualization; and, secondly, by providing a means of describing the tactics of implementation in terms of the resources or instructional management media necessary to accomplish the goal.

This paper is intended only as an introduction to instructional management. We have not detailed the strategies that would be included in the taxonomy, but have only highlighted a few of the more common ones. In describing the instructional management devices for media that may be employed, we have treated them as isolated devices. But each of these instructional management media (the teacher, the computer, the paraprofessional aide or the peer group member and the student himself) have some advantages and limitations. To the designer of instructional systems, the task will be to develop a total system which will incorporate the best instructional management and media mix. We expect the system of the future to be a combination of teacher, computer, proctor and student. The development of such a mix will be based on a general technology of instructional management which will result from continued research into strategies.

References

Bloom, B.S., Hastings, J.T. and Madaus, G.F. *Handbook on Formative and Summative Evaluation of Student Learning.* New York: McGraw-Hill, 1971.

Tosti, Donald T. and Ball, John R. A Behavioral Approach to Instructional Design and Media Selection. *AV Communication Review,* Spring, 1969.

Donald T. Tosti is Senior Vice President, Individual Learning Systems, San Rafael, California. **N. Paul Harmon** is an educational consultant, Palo Alto, California.

Classroom Management
of Learning Package Programs

Lucille W. Smith and Philip G. Kapfer

Learning packages, whether used in individualized settings or in group instructional situations, require student behaviors that usually differ from traditional expectations. For example, rather than simply reading from a textbook that is housed in the classroom, students may have to go to the library to use or check out trade books, reference books or non-print media. Instead of an entire class going to the library, accompanied by the teacher, an individual student or a small group of students may go to the library. Such seemingly simple changes in behavioral expectations can result in problems that actually undermine a teacher's confidence in a learning package program. Thus, the development of new behavioral competencies in students is extremely important to the success of a curriculum based on learning packages.

It is difficult, but not impossible, for a teacher who has had little experience with individualized learning package programs to visualize and anticipate new behavioral competencies that students must learn. Some of the behaviors and related factors that students must be able to deal with are the following:

1. Read (or listen to or look at) the learning package.
2. Follow the directions that are given.
3. Decide on what resources to use and what learning activities to do. Questions that eventually must be answered in order to make decisions about learning resources and activities include the following:
   a. Does the student need direct or mediated perceptual experiences with the subject matter of the

learning package?

b. Does the student need good descriptive reading material to help him vividly recall and verbalize about his prior perceptual experiences with the subject matter?

c. Does the student need to read and/or discuss ideas that are based on concepts he already has gained from his prior perceptual experiences with the subject matter?

d. Does the content of the learning package (e.g., symbolic material and operations, or motor skills) require practice for initial learning and for retention? How much? What sequence? With or without coaching and feedback?

4. Use the resources cited in the learning package and/or find own resources. Using or finding resources involves at least the following behaviors:

a. Go to where the resources are housed (in the school or in the community).

b. Locate the resources.

c. Use the resources (and check them out if necessary).

d. Operate any equipment that is required.

e. Return the resources.

f. Return to seat, classroom, work station, etc.

5. Decide, when sufficient learning has occurred, to use the learning in some way (e.g., in a written or performance test, in a project, etc.).

6. Follow standard operating procedures in the following settings:

a. Within the school.

b. Within the classroom.

c. When starting a learning package.

d. When using a learning package.

e. When completing a learning package.

Included in the above items are behaviors that can be classified under generic headings such as self-direction, respect for others, group cooperation, self-confidence, self-evaluation, leadership and self-initiative. An assortment of these behaviors in students is essential to the successful operation of learning package programs. Students typically do not have all of the behavioral competencies they need when they start learning package programs. In addition, these competencies are not the types of behaviors that can be developed rapidly. Therefore, it is well worth the time and effort to move slowly enough into a learning package program so that the competencies that are necessary to the success of the program can be developed. In fact, little of real significance in any educational program can happen anyway until opportunities are provided for the development of such competencies.

In all of the examples just described, teachers are dealing with students who range along a continuum of self-direction from a need for direct teacher monitoring to fairly complete student self-direction. Thus, one obvious competence that teachers must possess is the ability to diagnose where each student is in his individual development of each of these behaviors. In addition, the teacher must be able to identify progressively desirable behaviors in order to establish conditions that will increase the probability of successful performance by each student in a learning package program. Successive steps can then be taken by each student, and rewarded appropriately, so that the student can progress in the desired direction.

Because the authors in this issue focused on the philosophical, psychological and curricular bases for their particular learning packages, little space was devoted to helping teachers deal with the critically important implementation moves and strategies that mean the success or the failure of learning package programs. For this reason, the present article is addressed primarily to classroom teachers and to the very real problems they face in establishing and maintaining the obvious student behaviors that are necessary for making learning package programs function smoothly. Suggestions are also included for administrators and writers of learning package programs to promote effective classroom implementation.

Although the principles that we will describe have received

considerable attention elsewhere as they apply to numerous habit-type behaviors, we will illustrate the principles with examples from our experiences with classroom implementation of various types of individualized learning packages.

Three general classes of behavior will be considered. The first, which will be referred to as "facilitative behavior," is formed through the use of positive reinforcement techniques by the teacher in order to establish small "facilitative" commitments on the part of the student. Although such techniques do employ teacher-provided consequences in order to establish habit-type behaviors, the *natural consequences* of those behaviors, which eventually are perceived and conceptualized by the student, should ultimately lead to voluntary choice of those behaviors. The teacher's purpose in using reinforcement techniques is to promote habits of conforming to essential operating rules in return for the benefits the school provides. However, if these school benefits (which are the natural consequences just referred to) are not ultimately rewarding to the student, and teacher-provided consequences continue to be necessary, then the teacher had better take a good hard look at those supposed benefits—namely the curriculum content and processes with which the student interacts while using learning packages.

The second class of behaviors will be referred to as "disruptive behavior." When students are being shifted from existing learning modes to the use of learning packages, an atmosphere of uncertainty and confusion often exists. Students are not sure what is expected of them in the new setting. Old behaviors no longer meet classroom needs, and new behaviors have not yet been fully established. In such an atmosphere it must be expected that some children will react by engaging in disruptive behavior. These behaviors will be kept at a minimum if students know exactly *what* is expected of them, and are not expected to acquire new behavioral competencies at an unrealistic rate. If a good deal of disruptive behavior continues after new behavioral patterns have had a chance to develop, however, the teacher should look for weaknesses in the operation of positive reinforcement in the classroom and in the personal usefulness of the curriculum content to the students. If students feel good about themselves in relation to the school setting and to the curriculum content, then disruptive behavior should be at a very low level.

The third class of behavior, which is directly related to the natural consequences of conforming to essential operating rules, will be referred to as "self-motivated learning behavior." This kind of behavior is reinforcing because the various tasks in which the student engages result in the satisfaction of his wants, with learning contributing to that satisfaction. Such wants may be as simple and short range as satisfaction of curiosity, or as complex and long range as learning to fly an airplane, including the parts and functions of the airplane itself, rules and regulations of airports, the FAA and other agencies involved in flying, and both visual and instrument-controlled flight.

Developing Facilitative Behaviors

Considerable time in the early grades is spent establishing "acceptable" school behaviors. Children must learn, for example, to work and play cooperatively with other students and independently. They must learn to work quietly for extended periods of time and to talk productively at other times. Basic behavior modification techniques, which can be learned by teachers and applied with relative ease, are exceedingly powerful tools for establishing acceptable social behaviors as well as personal working habits which facilitate learning. However, as has already been stated, when shifting from traditional programs and materials to learning packages, additional behavioral competencies must be developed before children can be comfortable with the new style of learning. Steps in developing these behaviors are discussed in the following sections.

Select the Target Behavior

Before a behavior can be developed in students, the teacher must be able to state that behavior in a way that permits *observation and measurement* (Buckley and Walker,* pages 53-57). For example, a behavior that a teacher might want to develop is student self-checking of the pretest in a learning package. The behavior must be stated so that an observer can determine without doubt whether or not the objective is being met. The objective could be stated as follows: "After completing a pretest and being given an answer sheet by the teacher, the student will mark those questions missed and hand the answer sheet and marked paper to the teacher." An alternative statement could be as follows: "After completing a pretest, the student will (1) get the answer sheet from the file, (2) mark the questions he missed, (3) correct his answers as necessary, (4) return the answer sheet to the file and (5) place the corrected paper in his personal work file." In either event the specific target behavior is clear to anyone reading the statement, including the student.

Break Target Behavior into
Manageable Units
    Although the target behavior may be the same for all students, the units of smaller behaviors which make up the target behavior must be individually matched to each student (Buckley and Walker, pages 13-17). Since a teacher is usually dealing with a class of 20 or more students having individual capabilities, it is unrealistic to expect all students to achieve the same behavioral objective at the same time.
    In the example given above, the behavioral objective has five steps which make up the target behavior desired: (1) obtain the answer sheet from the file, (2) mark the questions missed, (3)

*The Buckley and Walker book will be cited whenever appropriate in this chapter. Our purpose for citing it is not to document the chapter, but rather to suggest one possible self-instructional source to which interested persons can turn for further study. A complete citation is as follows: Nancy K. Buckley and Hill M. Walker. *Modifying Classroom Behavior: A Manual of Procedure for Classroom Teachers* (1970), Research Press Company, Champaign, Illinois. A second source is: Mark L. Berman (Ed.), *Motivation and Learning: Applying Contingency Management Techniques* (1971), Educational Technology Publications, Englewood Cliffs, New Jersey.

correct the answers as necessary, (4) return the answer sheet to the file and (5) place the corrected paper in a personal work file. For one student the target behavior in its entirety might be a manageable unit of behavior. For another student a manageable unit might be just to place the corrected pretest into his own file. The smallest unit of behavior must be added to in small, incremental steps until the target behavior is reached. The teacher must take into consideration a given student's current behavior habits and his capacity for change before setting up a behavior modification program for that student.

Select a Reinforcer

A reinforcer is something that follows a behavior that makes the person feel good. By giving a reinforcer immediately following a student's desired behavior, the teacher assures that the behavior will increase in frequency (Buckley and Walker, pages 6-8). One of the reinforcers used most frequently by teachers is praise. This is effective with students who want teacher approval and who feel good when they receive it. Sometimes, however, more tangible reinforcers are needed in the beginning. For example, kindergarten children are sometimes given a gold star each time they remember to raise their hand before speaking in a group. An elementary student who finishes an assignment in a mathematics learning package might be allowed to check his answers on an electronic calculator. The novelty of using the calculator might motivate him to complete the learning task. Older children might also be given points each time they follow correct procedures in completing a learning package. These points might then be traded for free time in the library, a chance to play a game with another student, or the right to be a classroom helper for a period of time. High school students might prefer free access to the gym or time to work on individual projects. When using tangible reinforcement, praise should be given along with it. If this is done consistently, praise will become reinforcing by itself and tangible reinforcement programs can then be reduced. In any case, reinforcers must be matched to the wants and needs of individual students. What is reinforcing to one student may not be reinforcing to another.

Set Up a Schedule of Reinforcement

In order for a reinforcer to be effective it must be given IMMEDIATELY following the behavior that is wanted. It is also important that the behavior be reinforced EVERY TIME IT OCCURS until the behavior is established (Buckley and Walker, pages 30-31). In order for reinforcement to be effective, it must be given in such a way that the student associates the reinforcement with the behavior that is being developed. The most effective way for this to be accomplished is for the reinforcement to be given immediately following each and every occurrence of the behavior. After the behavior is fairly stable, the reinforcement can be gradually decreased until only occasional reinforcement is necessary. In this case, if reinforcement is given at irregular intervals, the behavior tends to be maintained at a high level.

Suppose the teacher wants to establish the behavior in students of independently retrieving reference material needed for a learning package. When the behavior is first being developed, the child is reinforced every time he successfully retrieves his own reference material. When the behavior is occurring consistently, the teacher begins spacing the reinforcement so that the child does not know in advance when he will be reinforced for the behavior. In order for the behavior to become permanently established, however, the student must see the usefulness of the behavior so that its occurrence is not dependent upon praise or other types of reinforcement programmed by the teacher. If the completion of the learning package itself is reinforcing, then all of the behaviors leading to the completion of the learning package (including independent retrieval of reference material) need not be reinforced after they have been initially established.

Eliminating Disruptive Behaviors

Disruptive behavior is defined as any student behavior which seriously interferes with the learning that is taking place in the classroom. Disruptive behavior ranges from daydreaming, which disrupts the learning of only one student, to physical aggression, which can disrupt the learning of the entire class. It should be kept in mind that direct control of disruptive behavior should be used sparingly and only as a temporary measure while acceptable classroom behaviors are being developed. Teachers, of course, strive to develop positive feelings about school and learning. This is generally more effectively done through the reinforcement of acceptable behaviors than through the control of disruptive behaviors. However, steps for dealing specifically with disruptive behaviors that do necessitate immediate action are discussed in the following sections.

Identify Target Behaviors

Before a behavior can be controlled, the teacher must be able to state that behavior in a precise way that permits observation and measurement (Buckley and Walker, pages 53-57). The teacher should be able to state what specific behavior is disruptive. It is not enough to say that Johnny disturbs the class; the teacher should know exactly what it is that Johnny does that disturbs the class.

Identify Uses and Reinforcers of
Disruptive Behaviors

It is generally agreed that all behavior has a purpose and that behavior is maintained because it helps a person achieve his goals (Buckley and Walker, pages 19-22). For example, a child does not fight with another child unless it satisfies some personal want or need. The attention he gets from the teacher may make him feel good, even though the attention may come in the form of punishment. On the other hand, fighting may result from a need to escape from an uncomfortable situation. Therefore, it is important for the teacher to find out, if possible, what specific things seem to contribute to a disruptive behavior. The teacher will usually get his best cues by observing what happens immediately before and after the disruptive behavior begins. If the teacher knows what triggers the behavior and what reinforces the behavior, he is in a much better position to deal with the target behavior by altering the contributing factors. For example, the target behavior may be Billy's hitting other students. The teacher may notice that hitting happens nearly every time Billy is given a new learning package in spelling to work on by himself, and that immediately following the hitting episode a general breakdown of class order occurs which delays the need for working on the spelling task. In this case, the teacher should examine the learning task to see if it is realistic for Billy, and evaluate the reinforcement schedule being used to establish Billy's self-directed behaviors in doing spelling packages.

Plan and Initiate a Program

There are at least four ways a disruptive behavior can be reduced or eliminated—by reinforcing incompatible behavior, by extinction, by "time-out" and by punishment.

1. Reinforcing Incompatible Behavior. *Some behaviors by their nature are incompatible with each other* (Buckley and Walker, page 44). For example, it is difficult for a student to write at the same time he is hitting another student. A person cannot sing and talk at the same time. He cannot look out the window and at the science interest center at the same time. Therefore, if the teacher can find an acceptable behavior that is incompatible with the disruptive behavior, consistent reinforcement of the acceptable behavior will of necessity lower the rate of the disruptive behavior. A teacher who is instructing his class in the use of harmonicas frequently finds that children blow the instruments at random while he is trying to give instructions. Therefore, he asks the students to hold their harmonicas above their heads while instructions are being given. As the children begin raising their harmonicas they are promptly given praise for following directions. Soon all harmonicas are being held high and the teacher can give the necessary directions without distraction.

2. Extinction. *Extinction means to remove the reinforcer that is maintaining a behavior. When the reinforcer is removed, the behavior is no longer useful and is gradually abandoned* (Buckley and Walker, pages 38-40). Application of this principle assumes, of course, that the reinforcer is apparent to the teacher, and that he can effectively remove it. In actual practice, however, it is extremely difficult to identify what is reinforcing a given behavior because there is often a combination of reinforcers and the

reinforcers may change over time. For example, in the elementary grades, students often misbehave apparently to get attention from the teacher. If the attention is not forthcoming, the misbehavior lessens. As children get older, however, there appears to be more need for peer attention, so that disruptive behavior may be wholly or partially reinforced by the reaction of other students in the classroom. Obviously, a particularly careful analysis and handling of contributing factors is required in the latter case.

3. "Time-Out." *"Time-out" means to remove the person from a condition where positive reinforcement is possible* (Buckley and Walker, pages 41-43). This method of controlling disruptive behavior can be used if there is a place where the student can be isolated from the rest of the class. A small room without stimuli of any kind is necessary if the student is to be truly removed from any possible reinforcement. When disruptive behavior occurs, the child is placed without comment into the time-out room, where he stays until he has remained quiet for a predetermined period of time, such as one minute. In no case should time-out exceed ten minutes, unless being employed by a highly trained expert in behavior modification. When the child is permitted back into the classroom, again no comment is made about the time-out. Some children, however, are imaginative enough to entertain themselves when completely alone, and may even like the solitude. Thus, the teacher must know his students and be able to predict how they probably will react before using time-out as a method of controlling behavior.

4. Punishment. *Punishment, when used in the context of behavior modification, can be anything that follows a behavior that makes the person feel bad. By using some form of punishment following a student's disruptive behavior, the teacher helps assure that the same behavior will decrease in frequency, at least temporarily* (Buckley and Walker, pages 32-37). One of the punishments most frequently used by teachers is verbal scolding. This is effective when a student wants teacher approval. Sometimes, however, *any* attention from the teacher is reinforcing and tends to increase the disruptive behavior rather than decrease it. In any case, most kinds of punishment typically control the

disruptive behavior only temporarily, and then only when the punishing agent is present. Johnny may refrain from fighting while in the teacher's presence, knowing that if he fights he will be sent to the principal's office, but fighting goes on at a high level when the teacher is not present.

If some kind of program is designed to decrease disruptive behavior, it is important that desirable behavior be reinforced during the same period. Most people would rather have approval than disapproval, and so will behave in acceptable ways if the desired behavior is reinforced. When desirable behavior is taken for granted and disruptive behavior gets attention, children will use disruptive behavior in order to get attention. Therefore, in the classroom the emphasis should always be on reinforcing desirable behavior. Punishment should only be used as an emergency measure and not as a continuing classroom management technique.

Self-Motivated Learning

We have been discussing the management of behaviors that either facilitate or impede learning in the classroom. The main purpose of school, of course, is to engage students in meaningful activities that result in significant learning. The principles of behavior modification that have been presented thus far work very effectively in the development of facilitative behaviors and in the elimination of disruptive behaviors. The same principles also are used with some success in "motivating" learning. For example, reinforcements in the form of good grades, praise, honor roll listings, etc., are dispensed regularly in school for completing learning tasks.

Any type of reinforcement that is programmed by the teacher or the school, however, will be discontinued eventually (for example, when the student leaves school). Thus, the student must perceive some intrinsic value to learning, or self-motivated learning will not develop. Clues to establishing self-motivated learning can be found outside of school and then applied to the school environment.

One of the kinds of learning in which people engage

throughout their lives results from exploring the environment. People look at things, feel them, touch them, smell them and taste them simply because real things are interesting. People interact with others and even interact with themselves. They observe and participate in events. And they observe and experience the consequences of their own behaviors and that of others. All of these concrete experiences are stored in the brain and are thought about, consciously or subconsciously, as the individual organizes his experiences into highly individualistic ideas. These cognitive memories, together with how the person feels about them, are each person's basis for his knowledge about the world. This knowledge is used each time the person must make a choice. Some choices are made with very little thought, such as grabbing a hamburger for lunch, while other choices are made only after becoming informed about and carefully weighing the alternatives. Once a choice has been made, it is carried out and consequences are experienced. In the simple example of selecting clothing to wear for skiing, if the person is cold all day because of his choices, he has a bad feeling, and this concrete experience becomes a part of his stored ideas and feelings. It affects his choosing behaviors the next time he is deciding what to wear for skiing.

What has just been described is a cycle of learning behavior, each part of which goes on continuously and constantly, but which does exhibit a sequential relationship among the parts. Experiences and their consequences constantly cause people to modify their own behavior. The natural rewards and punishments of behavior *are natural* because they result from the behavior and not from someone else's (e.g., the teacher's) imposition of consequences that normally would not have occurred without intervention.

Natural learning also can occur in school. The *interesting nature* or the immediate *usefulness* of what was learned can and should be the consequence, rather than rewards or punishments meted out by teachers. (In the latter case, where teacher-provided consequences are occurring, learning is going on, of course, but the learning is not necessarily what is prescribed by the learning materials, whether in the form of learning packages or not. Rather, the student may just be learning what turns the teacher on and off.)

Teachers or package writers can promote greater self-motivated learning in at least two ways when preparing and using learning packages. First, they can make sure that the learning activities in the package include experiences with concrete, real things that are available, or can be made available, in the school or in the community. (If such experiences are prerequisites for use of a learning package, care should be taken that students have these experiences *before* they pick up the package.) When a learning package is mediated with real things, the *interest appeal* of the package is increased. Second, the content of learning packages can be related, whenever possible, to situations in which the content that is to be learned can be applied immediately. The application must be realistic. Simulation games are fine if the real thing is impossible. The important point, in either case, is that the usefulness of a specified skill be immediate, real and motivating.

It may be a long time before all of the administrative, resource and community support systems teachers need are available, thus permitting learning to occur in its most natural context—through the use of self-motivated learning tasks. However, learning packages are a move in that direction. They do allow for individual decisions, the expression of individual preferences and the exercise of individual self-direction. Teachers and students should attempt to change from the present mode of instruction to self-motivated learning just as fast as practicality will allow. The final goal, however, should be kept in mind as transitional steps from traditional to individualized programs are taken: when learning packages can be used as an aid in helping the student find out information that he really wants to know to satisfy a personal need, then the natural reinforcement provided by the environment will replace many of the artificial reinforcements *presently* needed to control student behavior and learning.

Lucille W. Smith is a member of the SPURS Project Curriculum Design Team, Western States Small Schools Project, Salt Lake City. **Philip G. Kapfer** is with the Bureau of Educational Research, University of Utah, Salt Lake City.

DATE DUE

N. Dunathan			
DEC 14 '75			
DEC 5 '76			
DEC 18 '77			
GAYLORD			PRINTED IN U.S.A.